T0326410

Neuromarketing in food retailing

Neuromarketing in food retailing

edited by: Elena Horská and Jakub Berčík

Wageningen Academic
P u b l i s h e r s

EAN: 9789086863006
e-EAN: 9789086868438
ISBN: 978-90-8686-300-6
e-ISBN: 978-90-8686-843-8
DOI: 10.3921/978-90-8686-843-8

First published, 2017

© **Wageningen Academic Publishers**
The Netherlands, 2017

Wageningen Academic Publishers,
P.O. Box 220, 6700 AE Wageningen,
the Netherlands,
www.WageningenAcademic.com
copyright@WageningenAcademic.com

This book has been co-funded by the Erasmus+ programme of the European Union 'Food Quality & Consumer Studies' (Strategic partnership Erasmus + Nr. 2014-1-SK01-KA203-000464).

The European Commission support for the production of this publication does not constitute an endorsement of the contents which reflects the views only of the authors, and the Commission cannot be held responsible for any use which may be made of the information contained therein.

Book reviewers:
Andrzej-Krasnodębski
University of Agriculture in Krakow, Poland
Lukáš Stajanča
IBM ISC s.r.o., Data Analyst, Bratislava, Slovakia

Table of contents

Preface

This book is based on qualified contributions of experts in the field of marketing, neuromarketing and new technologies used in food retailing, services and marketing communication. All the chapters are outcomes of international project cooperation within Erasmus + Strategic partnership project 'Food Quality & Consumer Studies' started in 2014 with the aim to modernize and improve the quality of university education in the field of food science, food marketing and consumer studies, applied through the synergic effect of international cooperation, transfer of innovation and creation of new values in project consortium of 10 partners from 9 EU countries.

Project in the form of international mobility and training activities as well as through transfer of knowledge and creation of new values has created a framework and conditions for the development and pilot implementation of 8 intellectual outputs focused on sensory studies, sensory and aroma marketing, neuromarketing for food retailing, augmented reality for food marketers and consumers, health, nutrition, food consumer trends and product development. Intellectual outcomes in three cases represent not only innovative, but an entirely new product in the field of education, which has not been used in the educational process at partner universities so far (aroma and sensory marketing, neuromarketing for food retailing, augmented reality for food marketers).

I believe that this book 'Neuromarketing in food retailing' will provide readers from academic community and business sphere (university students, scholars, professionals) with with theoretical knowledge necessary for an in-depth understanding of neuromarketing issues at the level of theory and practical implications for food sector.

Publishing of the book has been co-funded by the Erasmus+ programme of the European Union 'Food Quality & Consumer Studies' (Nr. 2014-1-SK01-KA203-000464). I would like to thank all project team members working intensively during project period (2014-2017), especially authors of different chapters, reviewers as well as all those who in any way contributed to the content, or formal aspect of the book.

Elena Horská
Head author and project coordinator

1. Essential terminology of neuromarketing

J. Berčík

Slovak University of Agriculture in Nitra, Faculty of Economics and Management, Department of Marketing and Trade, Tr. A. Hlinku 2, 949 76 Nitra, Slovak Republic; jakubstudio@gmail.com

Abstract

Neuromarketing is a relatively young discipline that combines knowledge of neuroscience, psychology, economics, and also information technology into one functional unit. The main objective of this newly developing discipline is to understand how the human brain reacts and responds to specific marketing incentives. Neuromarketing research includes the use of a variety of sophisticated techniques for measuring biometric and brain signals when examining consumer behaviour and creating marketing strategies in order to see whether marketing tools are working properly, thus minimizing the potential risk of failure in the target market. The novelty of neuromarketing tends to cause opposing views among people which are largely related to the number of available and relevant information. On the one hand it presents a wave of uncritical enthusiasm from progress, new technologies, and knowledge, on the other hand many prejudices, concerns, and criticism. It can be assumed that criticism and concerns will subside over time and this young discipline will become socially accepted, frequent and strongly trended which will bring many interesting findings in the field of consumer behaviour and marketing management in the future.

Keywords: neuromarketing, consumer neuroscience, marketing

Learning objectives

After studying this chapter you should be able to:
► Describe and understand the concept of neuromarketing and its importance
► Understand how emotions, memory and senses work

1.1 The brief history of neuromarketing

Scientific development in recent years brought an expansion of various multidisciplinary research methods to give answers to the various questions of a particular scientific field. The increased use of neuroscientific methods with the aim of better understanding of human behaviour in various situations has led to the creation of the term 'neuroculture' (Frazzeto and Anker, 2009), which refers to new scientific branches combining neuroscience with other scientific disciplines, arts or humanities, such as neurophilosophy (Churchland, 1989) or neurotheology (Ashbrook, 1984). Tallis (2011) came up with a more pejorative term 'neuromania' to describe a headlong rush by many scientific disciplines to embrace neuroimaging and explain all human phenomena in terms of brain activity.

Economists were amongst the first social scientists to recognize the potential of brain imaging research and neuroimaging in the economic and business disciplines with the development of neuroeconomics (Braeautigam, 2005; Camerer *et al.*, 2004; Fehr *et al.*, 2005; Glimcher and Rustichini, 2004; Kenning and Plassmann, 2005; Sanfey *et al.*, 2006; Zak, 2004). Neuroeconomics has the longest history among 'neuro' sciences. It is the study of the brain's role in decision-making, in comparison with neuromarketing which is an applied field of study of how the brain responds to marketing stimuli (Shaw *et al.*, 2010).

The biggest challenge of marketing since the beginning is the pursuit of understanding consumer desires and needs and creating their interaction. To put it simply, the aim of marketing is to make selling pointless, to know and understand the customer to the extent that the goods or services are sold without additional promotion because they perfectly meet market requirements (Nagyová *et al.*, 2014). Ideally, marketing shall prepare the customer for the purchase so its only task is to ensure the availability of a product or service. Peter Drucker with this statement indirectly predicted the need to use neuromarketing, as the main aim of neuromarketing is to decode the processes taking place in consumer minds, in order to determine their desires, wishes and hidden causes of their choice, offering opportunities to give them what they really want (Boricean, 2009).

Therefore, since ancient times marketers and traders are trying to search techniques and tactics to influence consumer behaviour and stimulate the demand for products. Creating effective strategies is conditional on a deeper understanding of customer perception and decision-making. This can be achieved only with the knowledge available in the field of neuroscience (Javor *et al.*, 2013; Pradeep, 2010).

In the last ten years neuroscience has been applied not only in medicine, but also in marketing. Neuromarketing is another sophisticated field of marketing research that allows recognizing customer attitudes in detail and identifying the reasons why some behavioural processes occur. It is a broad term, unable to clearly define whether the respondent likes a stimulus or not. Nevertheless, by using different methods it is able to detect emotions, perceptions, memorability and attention devoted to the stimulus, as well as the impact of environmental factors. Based on this information the effect of the stimulus on the customer can be identified. That is also a reason why neuromarketing is at the forefront in the world of marketing, as it ensures more accurate results and companies which use neuromarketing are much more competitive than others (Berčík et al., 2014).

The most important reasons for the creation and development of this new tool in marketing can be considered the following:
- buyers are more sophisticated and overloaded with a greater amount of information;
- competition is more intense;
- the sales cycle is prolonged;
- resistance against traditional sales techniques is increasing.

Neuroscience research and findings about the human mind with its subconscious mechanisms shifted the interest towards the neuroscientific perspective of marketing, especially in the field of buying and advertising (Boricean, 2009; Morin, 2011; Shaw and Jones, 2009).

The first ideas of recording human brain activity appeared already in the 1970s when studying the impact of advertising on consumer behaviour. What is actually happening in the brain was mostly unknown until the 1990s despite initial neurotests. As a consequence, the research of sensorimotor, cognitive, and emotional reactions to various stimuli taking place in the human brain began at Harvard University (Lee et al., 2007). Here, Professor Gerry Zaltman was the first to use functional magnetic resonance imaging (fMRI) as a marketing research tool around 1999, thus suggesting further possibilities of using brain imaging technologies in marketing (Van der Sar, 2009).

Later, a report on the visual perception of Chrysler automobiles by scientists from the University of Ulm in Germany was presented (Erk et al., 2002), and a research to analyse the faces of presidential candidates by the University of California, Los Angeles, was partially financially supported from FKF Applied Research (Kaplan et al., 2007).

This sequence of gradually ongoing events (applying neuroimaging techniques in marketing) made it possible to create space for merging two scientific disciplines and thus shaping a new field – neuromarketing (Světlík, 2012).

Nevertheless, Professor Ale Smidts is considered to be the father of neuromarketing. He won the Nobel Prize in Economic Sciences in 2002 and his work is the concept of neuromarketing, first pronounced in the same year (Fandelová and Kačániová, 2012).

Despite the fact that the very concept of neuromarketing has been pronounced eleven years later, first researches in this field were developed in the United States already in 1991 (Figure 1.1). At first, there were the results of research laboratories specialized exclusively in neuroscience research. These studies were mainly carried out as a service for major companies. Although these research projects were initially confidential, cooperation with major companies (such as Coca-Cola, L-mart, Levi-Strauss, Ford, Delta Airlines) was further enhanced and the interest of these and other companies in neuromarketing was increasing.

Commercial neuromarketing research was first offered by US companies BrightHouse Institute for Thought Sciences and Salesbrain in June 2002. The new business division in BrightHouse was responsible for the practice of neuromarketing by using fMRI in marketing research and was immediately criticized for possible conflicts (Paul, 2002). The anti-advertising group Commercial Alert criticized the extent of promotion of fast food and they proposed the Federal Office for Human Research Protections in the U.S. Senate to investigate the Brighthouse study. As a result, their webpage was taken down (Canli,

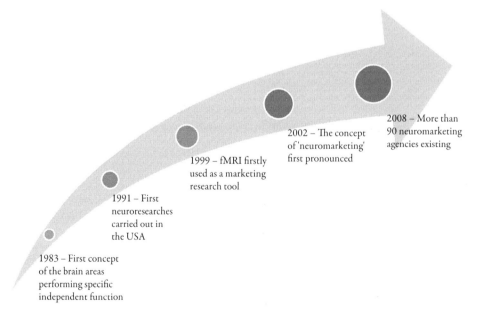

2008 – More than 90 neuromarketing agencies existing

2002 – The concept of 'neuromarketing' first pronounced

1999 – fMRI firstly used as a marketing research tool

1991 – First neuroresearches carried out in the USA

1983 – First concept of the brain areas performing specific independent function

Figure 1.1. Important milestones in the development of neuromarketing.

▸ finding real and true consumer preferences (i.e. seeking the 'buy button');
▸ subliminal influence (Zurawicki, 2010).

Neuromarketing is usually understood in the narrower sense only as a measurement of brain response to a marketing stimulus, but in the wider sense it includes also changes in physiological variables (e.g. heart rate or skin conductance measurement) (Nagyová *et al.,* 2014). The common characteristic is that neuromarketing is an area that combines the latest brain research on the border of:

▸ sales;
▸ marketing; and
▸ communication techniques (Renvoisé and Morin, 2007).

In the broader view of neuromarketing, there are three main ways that help us understand marketing and consumer behaviour better:

▸ It can provide information about what happens in the human brain during the action of marketing stimuli (any marketing stimulus in a controlled test).
▸ It can provide information about how the brain responds to marketing stimuli presented in different situational contexts (alone or alongside the competitive products, in various price categories, in the store compared to online sales, etc.).
▸ It can provide information about how the brain transforms these reactions into consumer behaviour and decision-making (buying a product or building loyalty to a new product).

As the primary benefit of this developing discipline may be considered the ground-breaking researches that explain how the brain comes to conclusions – consciously and subconsciously, and when it happens automatically, regardless of our logic. Step by step we are led through this discipline to understand the interaction between the old brain (manages the provision and implementation of basic physiological needs to survive) and the new brain (manages everyday decisions) (Figure 1.3).

The prefrontal emotional cortex creates emotions by producing hormones in the body. It is the youngest and flexible part of the brain. The postfrontal rational cortex can, on the other hand, only rely on rationality and analysis. The postfrontal cortex works independently in simple situations, however, the prefrontal cortex has to cooperate in more difficult ones (Georges *et al.,* 2014).

Tools that help to see into human brains and thus open the way to the psychological process of decision-making (the so-called black box of the brain) brought modern neuroimaging techniques used in neuroscience (Dooley, 2012). Some authors believe that neuromarketing is the application of neuroimaging techniques (mostly MRI – magnetic resonance imaging,

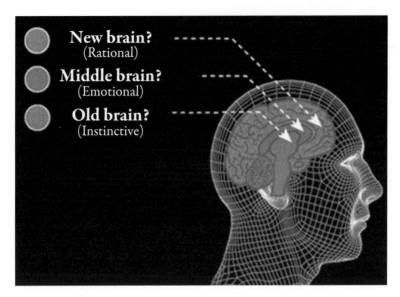

Figure 1.3. Identification of the parts of the human brain (based on Renvoisé and Morin, 2007, pp. 6).

fMRI – functional magnetic resonance imaging, MEG – magnetoencephalography, EEG – electroencephalography) mediated by a specific response of the cerebral cortex in order to analyse and understand human behaviour in relation to the market and market changes (Tolon *et al.*, 2008). Today the methods of neuromarketing research are already specific and non-invasive, hence neuroimaging technologies have become common practice when studying consumer behaviour (Lee *et al.*, 2007).

The first idea of the parts of the human brain performing exact mental functions was replaced by many different approaches of neuropsychology scientists, such as Sigmund Freud (the idea of psychoanalysis), or Lukas Teuber and Norman Geschwind (claiming all areas of knowledge relying on the functioning of the brain, with nothing to prevent the use of neuropsychology in fields like economics, aesthetics, pedagogy, or theology). At the same time, the 'neuro' prefix was added to many disciplines never before associated with brain mechanisms (Legrenzi and Umiltá, 2011).

Currently neuromarketing is usually associated with the commercial application of neuroscientific knowledge and tools that companies use in order to understand consumer responses to different kinds of brands, products, and services better, as well as the related communication effort. Thus many academic researchers think that the term has a bad reputation as a result of several cases of improper use of neuroscience methods and knowledge within their commercial use. For this reason, some scholars prefer the alternative term 'consumer neuroscience', in order to better reflect the academic approach to the application of neuroscience methods into studies of consumer behaviour and thinking.

(Hubert and Kenning, 2008)

There are misconceptions that neuromarketing is a discipline dealing with influencing (stimulating) people to buy goods – often those they do not need, and that therefore it is a socially unacceptable thing. The reason is partly its name – the term sounds contradictory, seemingly as a different type of marketing. This idea can be clarified through the following explanation:

▶ Marketing is a field aimed at influencing people to like products, which they buy in the end, including products that they may not need. Marketers are fully aware of the ongoing brain processes and associations, therefore marketing is and will always be loyal to influencing human brains.

▶ Neuromarketing is a new way of measuring the proper functioning of marketing. Neuromarketers believe that it is a better way of measuring marketing efforts because it is based on a more realistic understanding of how the consumer brain works.

Moreover, academicians have an obligation to provide information clearly and are responsible for transparency and correctness. Legal and ethical issues in neuroimaging research possibly causing issues might include human subjects' protection, medical privacy, and the public communication of research results (Kulynych, 2002).

However, neuromarketing with due respect for fundamental ethical principles does not present any threat. In fact, it is just a different type of market research that is subject to the same limitations of time, money and utility as any other type of normally carried out research (Genco *et al.*, 2013).

1.3 The importance of neuromarketing

Predicting consumer behaviour has always been a major interest of marketing experts. Traditional marketing researches are still effective and shall be used in marketing. However, there are situations when it is necessary to complement conventional methods by modern ones. Marketing experts say that marketers shall no longer be guided by what the respondents declare about themselves in surveys, because their brain – the part that does not pretend anything – often contradicts it (Gang *et al.*, 2012).

The basis of any successful business is market research, which can be defined as the systematic identification, collection, analysis, and evaluation of information related to a particular problem of a company (Malý, 2008). The three most commonly used methods in traditional marketing research include:

▸ interviews;
▸ group discussions (focus groups); and
▸ consumer questionnaires.

These methods have two important attributes in common: they are based on verbal self-assessment of people (what people say) in order to identify their attitudes, preferences and behaviour, and depend on people's ability to remember what exactly they were doing or thinking in the past. These traditional marketing researches are often effective, but there are situations where direct measurement has to be applied to obtain reliable information, using the techniques and methods used in neuroscience (Jedlička, 2011).

For several decades the most widely used method of marketing research is a questionnaire survey. |This type of research, however, reflects only the conscious perception of people (Vysekalová *et al.,* 2011). Factors that most often cause misstatements in traditional marketing research include:

▸ shortage of time;
▸ reluctance to answer honestly;
▸ subconsciousness of the person;
▸ misunderstanding of the research problem.

One of the reasons why it is necessary to supplement conventional research methods by modern ones is that brain activity and physiological changes in respondents as a response to various stimuli can provide marketers the information which is not part of conventional marketing research (Ariely and Berns, 2010). This is mainly due to the fact that people are not able to explain their preference if they are asked to do so, because human behaviour can be (and is) a managed process driven below the level of conscious perception (Calvert and Brammer, 2012; Gang *et al.,* 2012).

Neuromarketing research is based on the finding that 95% of human thinking and activity takes place in the subconscious (Kozel *et al.,* 2011). Generally, there are three major reasons that suggest the need to review subconscious reactions in consumer decision-making (Genco *et al.,* 2013):

▸ decisions are often based on subconscious processes and impacts;
▸ emotions strongly influence the decision-making – decisions are not made after careful and rational consideration of the impact of each option;

▸ decisions are not made after obtaining complete information, on the contrary, decision-making happens almost immediately and mostly right after receiving parts of the information available about the possible choices.

It means that even if people feel they have made a controlled, conscious, and fully informed decision, studies in recent decades have shown how these decisions actually deviate from what can be considered optimally rational. Consumer decision-making is often affected subconsciously (Figure 1.4) and rarely is a result of considering all options. This suggests the need for understanding the preferences of people in new, different ways than with just traditional research techniques.

Despite the fact that neuromarketing offers a portfolio of research techniques and methods, which are based on more realistic assumptions, traditional researches shall be still used in marketing because they have a proven importance and provide a good insight into the problem (e.g. interviews are indispensable for better understanding of consumer behaviour and brand perception) (Page, 2011).

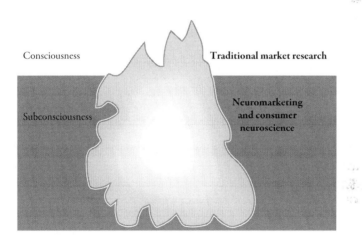

Figure 1.4. The iceberg analogy shows the differences between the traditional and neuromarketing market research (based on Ramsøy, 2015, pp. 18). The iceberg analogy shows how consumer neuroscience (neuromarketing) offers new ways for better understanding of the subconscious processes which are based on consumer behaviour. Since most mental processes operate subconsciously, traditional research methods such as interviews, surveys, and focus groups lag behind in addressing this aspect of consumer behaviour. Neuroscience tools and knowledge offer ways to allow better understanding of subconscious and conscious decision-making incentives of people.

The main advantages of traditional marketing research are:
► relatively low cost;
► easier processing and interpretation;
► does not require the presence of specialists (neurologists, psychologists);
► accepted by the general public;
► the availability of implementation.

The main advantages of neuromarketing research include:
► faster feedback;
► more detailed and accurate information (elimination of false information);
► finding real and true preferences;
► smaller representative sample of studied subjects;
► the use of the latest technologies.

Häusel (2006, pp. 10-12) also explains the advantages of neuromarketing as follows:
► Supremacy of the unconscious decision-making process, so neuromarketing can help understanding this process as well as the neural mechanisms which they are based on;
► Dominance of emotions and the emotional system structure over rational decisions;
► Multisensory processing in the brain through various channels of perception;
► Emotional-cognitive processing;
► Neurolinguistics – to help to optimize text and language;
► Neuroscientific personality research to identify certain customer types, which can accordingly be segmented with greater chance of success;
► Neuroscientific gender research where we can determine the effects of differences in thinking style, emotional structure, and behaviour for marketing purposes;
► Neuroscientific age research with regards to developing effective and efficient strategies to determine how aging consumers can be reached.

Nowadays marketers and companies can choose the method of obtaining information about target markets. They can choose traditional, neuromarketing or combined form of market research. The combination of traditional and neuromarketing research represents the best form of current market research, and therefore it is expected that neuromarketing research methods could become a common part of traditional researches in the future (Nagyová *et al.*, 2014).

Despite the fact that companies outwardly do not present this innovative form of research, attention is drawn at it by more and more companies and brands such as Camelot, Daimler Chrysler, Shopconsult, Heinz, Coca Cola, Levi-Strauss, Ford, Delta Airlines, Procter & Gamble, Motorola, Buick, GSK, Merck, Pfizer, McDonald's, Unilever, Intel, Viacom,

Johnson & Johnson, L'Oreal, Nestlé, Volkswagen, Google and many others (Boricean, 2009; Calvert, 2009; Davies and Harries, 2013).

Using neuromarketing can increase sales efficiency, in particular by:
► providing persuasive sales presentation;
► shortening the sales cycle;
► closing more business deals;
► creating effective marketing strategies;
► increasing revenues and profits;
► radically increasing the ability to influence others.

The essence of neuromarketing research lies in the fact that it comprehensively complements traditional marketing research and provides marketers complete answers mainly to three basic questions (Figure 1.5):
► What do people buy?
► How is the decision-making process going on?
► Why do people buy?

Neuromarketing is mainly about understanding how our brain works, regardless of the used methods, with a focus on improving the position of target products on the market. Key marketing areas in which neuroresearch methods can be applied include:
► brand (understanding and perception of the brand, branding);
► product (product innovation and packaging design);

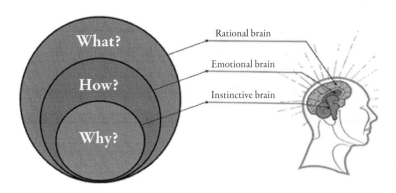

Figure 1.5. The construction of the brain from the viewpoint of evolution (based on Arjan, 2016).

- advertising (how advertising works, what makes a particular ad more successful than the others);
- shopping (visual and sensory stimuli and moving around the store);
- online (activation, persuading consumers);
- entertainment (engagement, the perception of television programs, films and video games) (Nagyová *et al.*, 2014).

Today, marketers are using neuromarketing in many research areas. Using a variety of techniques and technologies the following consumer responses can be measured:

- Implicit associations are connections in long-term memory, key to understanding impressions of novelty, familiarity, and processing fluency.
- Priming is the basic mechanism by which anything from our environment non-consciously influences our attitudes, goals, and behaviours.
- Attention is the brain mechanism by which nonconscious inputs get elevated to conscious awareness, its levels influence emotions, memory, and expectations.
- Discrete emotions, such as happiness, sadness, surprise, disgust, fear, anger, and contempt, are our universal emotional reactions.
- Emotional arousal and valence are dimensions of emotion. Arousal refers to level of stimulation, intensity, and agitation. Valence refers to direction of liking or disliking, positive or negative reaction.
- Approach and avoidance are the two nonconscious dimensions of motivation that drive action. They're motivational sources of attraction and aversion, heavily influenced by nonconscious, emotional conditioning (somatic markers).
- Memory activation is the extent to which memory encoding or retrieval is triggered by an experience.
- Value is the mental calculation of expected value, experienced value, and remembered value. It's derived from balancing loss aversion (cost, pain, inconvenience) with reward seeking (pleasure, benefit, payoff).
- Usability is the degree to which an online task is experienced as easy to do, efficient, and enjoyable. It's an attribute of web pages and websites.
- Preference is the judgement of value among alternative choice options.
- Choice is a key marketing outcome variable, a result of implicit or explicit decision-making measured directly by choice experiments.
- Behaviour and performance are additional important marketing outcome variables. Behaviours are outcomes of conscious and nonconscious mental processes, encompassing what people say or do. Performance is determined by measuring behaviour against a goal or expectation, resulting in a judgement of relative success or failure (Genco *et al.*, 2013, pp. 286-287).

The main benefit of this relatively young field of marketing lies in the enrichment of theoretical knowledge and in ensuring significant competitive advantage companies can gain by the proper application of information from neuroresearch activities. In developed countries, neuromarketing knowledge is used more frequently while it is applied to management, brand building, creating a strong position of the company and many other activities associated with developing effective marketing strategies. Due to increasing competitive pressures, attention shall be paid to improving the efficiency and success of business activities through creating more space for neuromarketing (Berčík, 2013).

1.4 The nervous system and the human brain

The nervous system is the main control, regulatory, and communication system based on the brain, spinal cord and nerves. The nervous system works on the principle of spreading the nerve impulse through nerve fibres (nerve pathways). The nervous system enables the communication of the body with the external and internal environment through receptors. The actual delivery of impulses is ensured by cells called neurons (Nagyová *et al.*, 2014).

Data in the form of electrical signals is relayed constantly between the sense organs and the brain, through complex networks of neurons and on a timescale measured in milliseconds (Carter *et al.*, 2014).

Neurons have three basic functions:
▶ sensory: transmit impulses from sensory organs to the central nervous system;
▶ connective (interneurons): process the received impulse;
▶ motoric: initiators of activities both controlled and not controlled by the will.

The nervous system has two parts:
▶ the central nervous system, consisting of the brain and spinal cord (CNS);
▶ the peripheral nervous system, consisting of nerves and neurons located beyond the central nervous system (PNS).

Within the CNS, the brain has 4 lobes, 3 layers, 2 hemispheres joined by one critical structure called the corpus callosum. The top layer called the cortex is the most recently evolved, the bottom part of the brain (the subcortical) is the most ancient. While the brain is fully formed at adolescence, the maturation of the circuitry is considered complete in the mid-twenties. The prefrontal cortex (PFC) is the last to mature, and it is a critical brain area for focus, attention, risk-assessment and working memory (Genco *et al.*, 2013; SalesBrain, 2016).

The purpose of the PNS is to connect the CNS to the limbs and other organs. It is a web of fibres and neurons, which communicates instructions, information, and alerts. It is divided into the somatic nervous system (SNS) and the autonomic nervous system (ANS). The SNS is the part of the PNS controlling voluntary movements through muscles, while the ANS is the part of the PNS responsible for the involuntary or visceral responses and affects heart rates, digestion, salivation, perspiration, pupillary dilation, and sexual arousal (Genco *et al.,* 2013; SalesBrain, 2016).

Since the CNS consists of the brain and spinal cord, neuromarketing is interested in this part when examining consumer behaviour, because the brain receives and evaluates all the stimuli coming from the external environment (Zurawicki, 2010).

The brain has a complex and many-layered anatomy. The set of structures within it includes some discrete masses, such as the cerebellum and thalamus, and zones of nerve fibres or nerve cells within large structures, discernible only by microscopic examination (Carter *et al.,* 2014).

The brain is 1,300-1,400 grams of mass consisting mainly of fat and water. The human brain is different from other brains by the frontal lobe that makes us civilized people. It allows us to manage well a variety of situations (emotionally, rationally, routinely, and innovatively), to survive as a species as well as individuals, and partly to be aware of living. The brain is fascinating as it contains more than 100 billion neurons, which create links encoded with all that we know and do. As these links are beyond the information possibilities offered by the DNA code, it is clear that the determining factor is what we encode in our brain in a certain way during our life based on stimuli from the environment. Fascinating is the fact that the brain operates as a dual-core processor, as it consists of two hemispheres (Švec, 2016).

The structure of the left and right cerebral hemispheres looks broadly similar. From the perspective of functionality, however, speech and language, reasoning and analysis, and certain communicating actions are based mainly on the left side in most people.

Since nerve fibres cross from left to right at the base of brain, this dominant left side receives sensory information from, and sends messages to, muscles in the right side of the body – including the right hand. Meanwhile, the right hemisphere is more concerned with sensory inputs, auditory and visual awareness, creative abilities, and spatial – temporal awareness (what happens in our surroundings, second by second) (Carter *et al.,* 2014).

The right hemisphere specializes in new situations (it is said to be the creative hemisphere) and represents the emotional (less rational) hemisphere. In general, women are more emotional than men and also that younger people have stronger emotional response compared to older people (Horská and Berčík, 2014).

The left hemisphere, on the contrary, specializes in routine and logic skills, including speaking, and can therefore be considered as a more rational hemisphere. Experiments with computer technology have shown that such differentiation significantly increases the 'computing' capacity of the processor and thus the brain. Both hemispheres are interlinked through bundles of axonal fibres known as the corpus callosum.

Stimuli from the right half-brain are processed in both hemispheres, while from the left half-space only by the right hemisphere. Stimuli captured with the right side of the brain are thus more effectively captured and processed. The right hemisphere addresses new ideas, the left uses learned routines. Too frequent use of routines causes loss of ability to solve phenomena perceived by the senses as creative.

The term 'brain' in the literature is often associated with anatomical structures or circuits forming the human brain. The term 'mind' is usually used to express the subjective cognitive brain conditions (e.g. prefrontal cortex is an anatomical part of the brain, but attention is a cognitive state of mind produced by brain activity) (Genco et al., 2013).

1.5 The emotions

Special attention in neurological perspective when examining consumer behaviour is dedicated to centres of creating emotions referred to as the 'emotional brain'. Emotional activity is most commonly associated with the activity of the limbic system, especially with its part – the amygdala, which is a key structure for determining the affective value of sensory and complex social stimuli. Another part is the cerebral cortex (neocortex), which acts on a different principle and performs different functions.

Emotions may seem to be conscious feelings, but they are in fact, inner motions – physiological responses to stimuli. They either push away from danger or towards reward. Emotions are generated constantly in the limbic system, which is a cluster of structures that lies beneath the cortex and in humans it is closely connected with the more recently evolved cortical areas. Emotions are consciously felt and conscious thoughts affect emotions. Each emotion is produced by a different network of brain modules, including the hypothalamus and pituitary gland, which control the hormones that produce physical reactions (e.g. increased heart rate and muscle contraction) (Carter et al., 2014).

Emotions can be characterized as complex experiencing of events and situations that are conditioned by the relationship between objective characteristics and needs of the subject based on the conscious and subconscious evaluation of a subjectively important situation (Vysekalová *et al.,* 2014).

The amygdala picks up on emotional stimuli even before we are aware of them, enabling the body to react very quickly to the threat or reward. Emotional stimuli are processed along a second route that does not involve the amygdala. This takes the information through cortical areas that produce conscious awareness and a more thoughtful response (Carter *et al.,* 2014).

Emotions can be classified not only according to what feeling they cause, but also by their quality and the length of their duration. The basic classification of emotions lies in their division into positive and negative ones. It should be noted that when considering the impact of marketing stimuli on the emotional involvement of the researched subjects a negative emotion is also a relevant answer for marketing experts. The classification of emotions according to different authors varies, but the most frequent include fear, anger, sadness, and happiness, quite often named are also disgust and surprise.

Emotions according to their duration can be divided into:
▸ Affects: sudden and significantly ongoing, intensive, short-term emotional reactions to various experiences. They are characterized by rapid formation, turbulent course, short duration and lack of rational control in actions.
▸ Moods: express more permanent readiness of emotional reactions. They are characterized by low intensity and longer duration. They influence the degree of other mental functions such as attention, memory, motivation, behaviour, interests, and attitudes.
▸ Long-term emotional relations: long-lasting permanent feelings that are specifically targeted to a particular object or activity. These are very intense emotions (e.g. passions) that influence the actions of the person.

Emotions can be further divided according to their quality to lower (joy, sadness, fear, anger, etc.) and higher (intellectual, aesthetic, social, etc.). Lower emotions are mostly associated with the instincts and impulses (e.g. hunger, thirst). Higher emotions are sometimes referred to as moral feelings, because they are part of the ethical, aesthetic, social, and intellectual attitudes and actions.

1.6 The memory

Although emotions are linked to all mental processes, their closest relation is towards motivation, memory and learning.

In the relation of emotions and learning, emotions largely influence what one learns, determine the choice of means and objectives. Motivation is often of emotional origin and emotions tend to be the impulse for the activities of individuals. Similar to emotions, memory is the subject of several studies and the relation between them is not simple. Memory means the ability to store structured information in time and is represented by the processes of inculcation, storage, and handling information.

The human brain is equipped with different types of memory, each of which is characteristic by specific neuronal ties:

▶ Sensory memory: allows to store sensory inputs long enough to be processed by the brain, which takes less than one second.
▶ Short-term memory: allows keeping small amount of information in mind, usually for not more than a minute, until the thing is being considered.
▶ Long-term memory: stores the memories of more distant past, including things learned and experiences. Only this memory is important for branding. Long-term memory has a different architecture composed from two subsystems – from the explicit and implicit memory.
▶ Episodic memory: records the everyday episodes of our lives. Although we cannot remember everything, the most important personal moments we remember for a lifetime (e.g. the wedding day, first day in work, the day we were awarded, etc.) (Sharma *et al.,* 2010). Rather than merely referring to the experience at the time, it reminds about the mental state, mostly associated with emotions.
▶ Procedural memory: records the necessary aspects of various actions or keeps ways how to perform various activities (e.g. driving a car, cycling or making tea).
▶ Semantic memory: refers to the knowledge of facts and the world. This is an encyclopaedic and descriptive knowledge that may not be based on personal experience. This category includes simple data and symbols (e.g. brands, logos, prices). This memory also allows raising expectations before the event, to ensure better memorability for the future (Zurawicki, 2010).

Remembered value refers to how different brand associations are encoded, stored and retrieved in the memory, while parts of these processes happen on an unconscious level (similarly as in consumer psychology). For example, Van Osselaer and Janiszewski (2001) distinguished between the Human Associative Memory model, a process that was a general and unfocused incidental (or unconscious) associative learning, and an adaptive learning mechanism focusing on feature-benefit associations for future rewards. Hence, the remembered value consists of both explicit and implicit memory of prior consumption experience (Plassmann *et al.,* 2012).

The human brain is able to consciously accept and process much less information than it gets from the external environment. The opposite of the conscious perception is the subconscious perception of our mind, which provides all the vital functions of our body while it records things people learned, even if they are not aware of it. The subconscious perception allows capturing many sensory stimuli, which can be perceived simultaneously with the information perceived consciously. The paradox is that while the conscious perception occurs only through one channel, the subconscious perception takes place through multiple channels at the same time. Consciousness is linked with attention. Information are perceived consciously and registered at the same moment they were captured (e.g. when we notice the price of the product exhibited on supermarket shelves or in store displays). Stimuli perceived subconsciously can be stored in the memory similarly as the reactions of consciously processed stimuli (Nagyová *et al.,* 2014).

1.7 The senses

The brain reaches out to the environment through our sense organs, which respond to various stimuli including light, sound waves, and pressure. The information is transmitted as electrical signals to the cerebral cortex to be processed into sensations such as vision, hearing, and touch (Carter *et al.,* 2014).

The moment when consumers make their decisions is largely influenced by what they see, hear, feel, and touch in their surrounding environment, because there are immediate signals for creating emotions (Kang *et al.,* 2011).

The customer's senses are the doors to the brain and purchase decisions, therefore special attention must be paid to satisfying the customer's nose, ears, eyes, and skin while entering through all doors at once.

The nose, ears, and touch are as important as the eye, as these more primary senses give access to less conscious decisions, less controlled by reason. The olfactory nerve, for example, has a direct and priority link to the limbic lobe, which is the pleasure and memory centre (Georges *et al.,* 2014). Up to one quarter of the human brain is involved in visual processing, far more than with any other sense (Pradeep, 2010).

References

Ariely, D. and Berns, G.S., 2010. The hope and hype of neuroimaging in business. Nature Reviews Neuroscience 11(4): 284-292.

Arjan, E., 2016. Neuroscience of online engagement – Excerpt. Available at: http://tinyurl.com/k4b9paw/.

Ashbrook, J.B., 1984. Neurotheology: the working brain and the work of theology. Zygon Journal of Religion and Science 19(3): 331-350.

Berčík, J., 2013. The modern forms of marketing research in selected agri-food businesses. In: Horská, E. and Ubrežiová, I. (eds.) Business management – Practice and theory in the 21st century: international scientific conference: proceedings of scientific papers. Slovak University of Agriculture in Nitra, Nitra, the Slovak Republic, pp. 154-161.

Berčík, J., Paluchová, J., Kleinová, K., Horská, E. and Nagyová, Ľ., 2014. Stimulus, space and hidden customer's reactions: applying possibilities of neuromarketing. In: Zentková, I. (ed.) Improving performance of agriculture and the economy: challenges for management and policy. Book of Abstracts of the International Scientific Days 2014, 13th International Conference. May 21-23, 2014, High Tatras, Slovak Republic, 138 pp.

Boricean, V., 2009. Brief history of neuromarketing. In: ICEA – FAA (ed.) Proceedings of the International Conference on Economics and Administration. University of Bucharest, Bucharest, Romania, 2009, pp. 119-121.

Braeutigam, S., 2005. Neuroeconomics – From neural systems to economic behaviour. 2nd Conference on NeuroEconomics – ConNEcs 2004. Brain Research Bulletin 67(5): 355-360.

Calvert, G.A. and Brammer, M.J., 2012. Predicting consumer behavior: using novel mind-reading approaches. IEEE Pulse 3(3): 38-41.

Calvert, G.A., 2009. Neuromarketing. Available at: http://tinyurl.com/n32ucsd.

Camerer, C.F., Loewenstein, G. and Prelec, D., 2004. Neuroeconomics: why economics needs brains. Scandinavian Journal of Economics 106(3): 555-579.

Canli, T., 2006. When genes and brains unite: ethical implications of genomic neuroimaging. In: Illes, J. (ed.) Neuroethics: defining the issues in theory, practice, and policy. Oxford University Press, Oxford, UK, pp. 169-193.

Carter, R., Aldridge, S., Page, M. and Parker, S., 2014. The human brain book. DK Publishing, New York, NY, USA, 264 pp.

Churchland, P.S., 1989. Neurophilosophy: toward a unified science of the mind/brain. MIT Press, London, UK, 560 pp.

Davies, S. and Harries, S., 2013. Neuromarketing mad scientists meet 'Mad Men'? DRAFTFCB, London, UK, 5 pp. Available at: http://tinyurl.com/llzzmte.

Dooley, R. et al., 2015. Neuromarketing careers. Available at: http://tinyurl.com/k9ttzqc.

Dooley, R., 2012. Brainfluence: 100 ways to persuade and convince consumers with neuromarketing. John Wiley, Hoboken, NJ, USA, 304 pp.

Erk, S., Spitzer, M., Wunderlich, A.P., Galley, L. and Walter, H., 2002. Cultural objects modulate reward circuitry. Neuroreport 13(18): 2499-2503.

Fandelová, E. and Kačániová, M., 2012. Analýza aktuálnych trendov marketingovej komunikácie – neuromarketing. 25 pp. Available at: http://tinyurl.com/k3p6fkm.

Fehr, E., Fischbacher, U. and Kosfeld, M., 2005. Neuroeconomic foundations of trust and social preferences: initial evidence. American Economic Review 95(2): 346/351.

Ferguson, R., 2009. Neuromarketing: what the human brain means to your campaign. Available at: http://tinyurl.com/k4386kz.

Frazzetto, G. and Anker, S., 2009. Neuroculture. Nature Reviews Neuroscience 10(11): 815-821.

Gang, D.J., Lin, W., Qi, Z. and Yan, L.L., 2012. Neuromarketing: marketing through science. International Joint Conference on Service Sciences (IJCSS): 285-289.

Genco, S.J., Pohlmann, A.P. and Steidl, P., 2013. Neuromarketing for dummies. John Wiley, Mississauga, Canada, 408 pp.

Gentner. F., 2012. Neuromarketing in the B-to-B sector: importance, potential and its implications for brand management. Diplomica Verlag GmbH, Hamburg, Germany, 82 pp.

Georges, P.M., Bayle-Tourtoulou, S. and Badoc, M., 2014. Neuromarketing in action: how to talk and sell to the brain. Kogan Page, London, UK, 280 pp.

Glimcher, P.W. and Rustichini, A., 2004. Neuroeconomics: the consilience of brain and decision. Science 306(5695): 447-452.

Häusel, H.-G., 2006. Neuromarketing. Erkenntnisse der Hirnforschung für Markenführung, Werbung und Verkauf. Rudolf Haufe Verlag GmbH & Co. KG, Niederlassung Planegg / München, Germany, 232 pp.

Horská, E. and Berčík, J., 2014. The influence of light on consumer behavior at the food market. Journal of Food Products Marketing 20(4): 429-440.

Hubert, M. and Kenning, P., 2008. A current overview of consumer neuroscience. Journal of Consumer Behaviour 7(4-5): 272-292.

Javor, A., Koller, M., Lee, N., Chamberlain, L. and Ransmayr, G., 2013. Neuromarketing and consumer neuroscience: contributions to neurology. BMC Neurology 13: 13.

Jedlička, P., 2011. Neurověda se uplatní I ve světě marketingu. Available at: http://tinyurl.com/m5b7fjw.

Kang, E., Boger, C.A., Back, K.-J. and Madera, J., 2011. The impact of sensory environments on Spagoers' emotion and behavioral intention. Available at: http://tinyurl.com/mxmryw7.

Kaplan, J.T., Freedman, J. and Iacoboni, M., 2007. Us versus them: political attitudes and party affiliation influence neural response to faces of presidential candidates. Neuropsychologia 45(1): 55-64.

Kenning, P. and Plassmann, H., 2005. NeuroEconomics: an overview from an economic perspective. 2nd Conference on NeuroEconomics – ConNEcs 2004. Brain Research Bulletin 67(5): 343-354.

Kozel, R., Mlynářová, L. and Svobodová, H., 2011. Moderní metody a techniky marketingového výzkumu. Grada, Prague, Czech Republic, 304 pp.

Krugman, H.E., 1971. Brain wave measures of media involvement. Journal of Advertising Research 11(1): 3-9.

Kulynych, J., 2002. Legal and ethical issues in neuroimaging research: human subjects protection, medical privacy, and the public communication of research results. Brain and Cognition 50(3): 345-357.

Lee, N., Broderick, A.J. and Chamberlain, L., 2007. What is neuromarketing? A discussion and agenda for future research. International Journal of Psychophysiology 63(2): 199-204.

Legrenzi, P. and Umiltá, C., 2011. Neuromania: on the limits of brain science. Oxford University Press, New York, NY, USA, 144 pp.

Lindstrom, M., 2009. Nákupologie: Pravda a lži o tom, proč nakupujeme. Computer Press, Brno, Czech Republic, 240 pp.

Malý, V., 2008. Marketingový výzkum: teorie a praxe. Oeconomics, Prague, Czech Republic, 181 pp.

Morin, Ch., 2011. Neuromarketing: the new science of consumer behavior. Society 48(2): 131-135.

Nagyová, Ľ., Horská, E., Kretter, A.,Kubicová, Ľ., Košičiarová, I., Récky, R., Berčík, J. and Holienčinová, M., 2014. Marketing. Slovak University of Agriculture in Nitra, Nitra, Slovak Republic, 460 pp.

Page, G., 2011. Lepší práce s mozkem – efektívní využití neurovědy. In: Du Plessis, E. (ed.) Jak zákazník vnímá značku: nahlédněte s pomocí neurovědy do hlav spotřebitelů. Computer Press, Brno, Czech Republic, pp. 139-148.

Paul, A., 2002. Brighthouse institute for thought sciences launches first 'neuromarketing' research company: company uses neuroimaging to unlock the consumer mind. Available at: http://tinyurl.com/mv79p7a.

Plassmann, H., Ramsøy, T.Z. and Milosavljevic, M., 2012. Branding the brain: a critical review and outlook. Journal of Consumer Psychology 22: 18-36.

Pradeep, A.K., 2010. The buying brain: secrets for selling to the subconscious mind. John Wiley and Sons, Hoboken, NJ, USA, 272 pp.

Ramsøy, T.Z., 2015. Introduction to neuromarketing and consumer neuroscience. Neurons Inc. ApS, Rørvig, Denmark, 204 pp.

Renvoisé, P. and Morin, Ch. 2007. Neuromarketing: understanding the 'Buy Buttons' in your customer's brain. SalesBrain, Thomas Nelson, Nashville, TN, USA, 256 pp.

SalesBrain, 2016. Neuro 101: getting started with neuromarketing. Available at: http://tinyurl.com/n38dk84.

Sanfey, A.G., Loewenstein, G., McClure, S.M. and Cohen, J.D., 2006. Neuroeconomics: cross-currents in research on decision-making. Trends in Cognitive Sciences 10(3): 108-116.

Sharma, J.K., Singh, D., Deepak, K.K. and Agrawal, D.P., 2010. Neuromarketing: a peep into customer's minds. PHI Learning Private Limited, New Delhi, India, 272 pp.

Shaw, C., Dibeehi, Q. and Walden, S., 2010. Customer experience. future trends and insights. Palgrave Macmillan, London, UK, 199 pp.

Shaw, E.H. and Jones, B.D.G., 2009. A history of schools of marketing thought. Marketing Theory 5(3): 239-282.

Singer, E., 2004. They know what you want. New Scientist 2458. Available at: http://tinyurl.com/l9zt7n4/.

Smidts, A., 2002. Kijken in het brein: over de mogelijkheden van neuromarketing. ERIM Inaugural Address Series Research in Management, EIA-12-MKT, 54 pp. Available at: http://repub.eur.nl/pub/308/.

Švec, M., 2016. Manipuluje neuromarketing? Available at: http://neuromarketing.sk/?p=667.

Světlík, J., 2012. O podstatě reklamy. Eurokódex, Bratislava, Slovak Republic, 312 pp.

Tallis, R., 2011. Aping mankind: neuromania, darwinitis and the misrepresentation of humanity. Acumen, Routledge, London, UK, 388 pp.

Thompson, J., 2005. They don't just want your money. They want your brain. Available at: http://tinyurl.com/n2xvngg.

Tolon, M., Özdoğan, F.B. and Eser, Z., 2008. Testing cognitive dissonance theory: consumers' attitudes and behaviors about neuromarketing. Muhan Soysal Business Administration Conference, Middle East Technical University, Northern Cyprus.

Van der Sar, M., 2009. Neuromarketing, a contribution to buzz a new product. Rotterdam University for Applied Science, Rotterdam, the Netherlands, 57 pp.

Van Osselaer, S.M.J. and Janiszewski, Ch., 2001. Two ways of learning brand associations. Journal of Consumer Research 28(2): 202-223.

Vysekalová, J., 2011. Chování zákazníka: jak odkrýt tajemství 'černé skříňky'. Grada, Prague, Czech Republic, 356 pp.

Vysekalová, J., 2014. Emoce v marketingu: jak oslovit srdce zákazníka. Grada, Prague, Czech Republic, 296 pp.

Whole-Brain Presenting, 2016. Available at: http://tinyurl.com/k59rrj4.

Williams, J., 2010. Neuromarketing – Add it to the marketing toolbox. Available at: http://tinyurl.com/lc6d4f8.

Zak, P.J., 2004. Neuroeconomics. Philosophical transactions of the Royal Society London (Biology) 359(1451): 1737-1748.

Zaltman, G. and Zaltman, L.H., 2008. Marketing metaphoria: what deep metaphors reveal about the minds of consumers. Harvard Business Review Press, Boston, MA, USA, 230 pp.

Zurawicki, L., 2010. Neuromarketing: exploring the brain of the consumer. Springer-Verlag, Berlin Heidelberg, Germany, 273 pp.

2. Interdisciplinary relations of neuromarketing and neuropsychology

J. Berčík

Slovak University of Agriculture in Nitra, Faculty of Economics and Management, Department of Marketing and Trade, Tr. A. Hlinku 2, 949 76 Nitra, Slovak Republic; jakubstudio@gmail.com

Abstract

The interdisciplinary field of research that analyses the behaviour of people in economic decision-making situations with the methods that monitor the activity of the nervous system has been strengthened since the beginning of the 21st century. This chapter provides an overview of the most important scientific concepts this relatively young discipline is based on. Each of them represents significant discoveries in brain sciences: neuroscience, psychology, behavioural economics and neuroeconomics, the contribution of which lies primarily in better understanding of how and why consumers act the way they do, what they like, how they choose and why they are buying.

Keywords: interdisciplinary research, psychology, neurology, economy

Learning objectives

After studying this chapter you should be able to:
- Understand various interdisciplinary relations of neuromarketing with other scientific disciplines

2.1 Integration of scientific disciplines

New approaches that integrate several disciplines such as economics, biology, psychology, neuroscience, etc. (Figure 2.1) are considered appropriate for providing better explanation of economic events and complex economies of today. Brain imaging research has a special place especially in the economic and business disciplines. Another new approach in comparison to conventional economic theory is neuroeconomics that studies the impact of emotional, social, psychological, and other factors on the various economic decisions and explains the principles of decision-making process and behavioural strategies of consumers based on neurobiological and psychological aspects. Additionally, marketing theory and practice use the application of neuroscience for better understanding of consumer choice and for influencing consumer behaviour (Horská *et al.*, 2015).

Linking interdisciplinary relations of cognitive sciences and neuroscience to marketing decision-making environment, and applying this knowledge in any area of marketing (e.g. package, research, and development of new products and services, marketing communications, merchandising) is called neuromarketing (Vysekalová *et al.*, 2011).

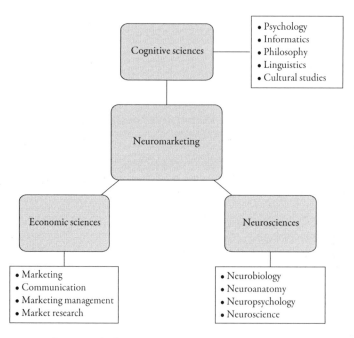

Figure 2.1. Neuromarketing – linking several scientific disciplines (based on Du Plessis, 2011, pp. 36).

After publishing the first neuroeconomic papers, the potential of neuroscientific methods beside the classical qualitative and quantitative methodologies in the social sciences was discovered. The term 'neuromarketing research' was suggested quite early in order to categorize interdisciplinary studies between economics, psychology, biology, and medicine (Smidts, 2002). However, multiple definitions appeared to develop, with the technological advances expanding an array of tools available to researchers in this field (Dawson *et al.*, 2000; Lee and Chamberlain, 2007; Ohme *et al.*, 2009).

Penenberg (2011) from the layman's perspective states that neuromarketing is a science (or perhaps even an art) that detects electrical signals from the brain and analyses brain reactions with a software and interprets them to marketing experts.

It is the brain that is responsible for the buying behaviour. However, in order for it to operate properly, it uses a lot of energy, though the brain itself constitutes only 2% of our body weight. Only 20% of our brain we use knowingly, which means that we do not control the substantial part of our attention. The brain is thus dependent on instinctive reactions. In terms of neuromarketing it means that on the basis of neuromarketing some specific principles were developed which are used for customizing marketing messages to customers (Morin, 2011).

According to Thompson (2005), 95% of our thoughts and emotions lie beneath the level of consciousness. Thus, the study of the brain can detect human emotions in a more detailed way than verbal expressions.

Breiter *et al.* (2015) explain the differences between neuroeconomics and neuromarketing. Neuroeconomics generally explains how the individuals make their choices and represents distribution of choices. There are four steps in the process of decision-making (choice disambiguation, identification and framing, valuation of choices, selection among choices and assessment of outcome). On the other hand, neuromarketing focuses on how individuals and groups can be shifted or altered from one pattern of decisions to another pattern, or to change their distribution of choices. One potential model for the effect of influence on behaviour is shown by Breiter *et al.* (2015) where influence can be considered the difference in gradients for preference inside a person and outside a person and behaviour feeds back onto these internal and external gradients of preference as experienced utility of expressed behaviour.

Research in the field of consumer neuroscience has generally been positively accepted within the academic community and included in the theories of marketing scholars, however, medicine is reluctant to adopt the results of consumer neuroscience. First attempts to transfer knowledge between neuroeconomics and psychiatry have been published (Sharp *et al.*, 2012), but a joint discussion of how consumer neuroscience knowledge can contribute to a broader field of science, including especially biology, neuroscience, psychiatry, and neurology, is still insufficient. Nevertheless, findings from these studies are significantly contributing to all behavioural sciences, mainly by focusing on the interaction of cognitions and emotions in human behaviour (Cohen, 2005; Shiv, 2007; Shiv and Fedorikhin, 1999).

2.2 Interdisciplinary relations with psychology

The question of how we make and how we shall make decisions and judgments interests philosophers for hundreds of years and still inspires some disciplines such as philosophy and some areas of psychology.

Biological psychology is a study of the physiological, evolutionary, and developmental mechanism of behaviour and experience. It is approximately synonymous with the terms biopsychology, psychology, physiological psychology, and behavioural neuroscience. The term 'biological psychology' emphasizes that the goal is to relate biology to issues of psychology. Neuroscience includes much that is relevant to behaviour but also includes more detail about anatomy and chemistry (Kalat, 2011).

The various specializations that are closely linked to biological psychology can be seen in Table 2.1.

Exceptional progress in mapping the brain started the growth of scientific disciplines such as neuropsychology, which is defined as understanding the functioning of our nervous system, as it studies the relationship between the human brain and cognitive and mental functions (Morin, 2011). Clinical psychology, which is more organically conceived, is often referred to as neuropsychology (Pribišová, 2007).

According to the American Psychological Association (APA, 2010), clinical neuropsychology is a specialty in professional psychology that applies principles of assessment and intervention based upon the scientific study of human behaviour as it relates to normal and abnormal functioning of the central nervous system. It is a comprehensive psychological discipline, overlapping at times with areas such as neuroscience, philosophy (particularly philosophy of mind), neurology, psychiatry, and computer science (particularly by making use of artificial neural networks). The specialty is dedicated to enhancing the understanding of brain-behaviour relationships and the application of such knowledge to human problems.

Table 2.1. Selected fields of specialization (Kalat, 2011, pp. 7).

Specialization	Description
Neuroscience	Studies the anatomy, biochemistry, or physiology of the nervous system
Behavioural neuroscience	Investigates how functioning of the brain and other organs influences behaviour
Cognitive neuroscience	Uses brain research, such as scans of brain anatomy or activity to analyse and explore people's knowledge, thinking, and problem solving
Neuropsychology	Conducts behavioural tests to determine the abilities and disabilities of people with various kinds of brain damage and changes in their condition over time
Psychophysiology	Measures heart rate, breathing rate, brain waves and other body processes and how they vary from one person/situation to another
Neurochemistry	Investigates the chemical reactions in the brain
Clinical psychology	Helps people with emotional problems
Neurology	Treats people with brain damage or diseases of the brain
Neurosurgery	Performs brain surgery
Psychiatry	Helps people with emotional distress or troublesome behaviours, using drugs or other medical procedure

Biological explanation of behaviour fall into four categories: physiological, ontogenetic, evolutionary and functional (Tinbergen, 1951). A physiological explanation relates behaviour to the activity of the brain and other organs. It deals with the machinery of the body – for example, the chemical reactions that enable hormones to influence brain activity and the routes by which brain activity control muscle contractions. An ontogenic explanation describes how a structure or behaviour develops, including the influence of genes, nutrition, experience, and their interactions. A revolutionary explanation reconstructs the history of a structure or behaviour (Shubin *et al.*, 2009) while a functional explanation describes how a structure or behaviour evolved as it did (Kalat, 2011).

Psychology in recent years focuses on the impact of subconscious processes in the human mind. It considers as the most important to understand how the conscious and subconscious processes in human activities cooperate in consumer behaviour and choice. For this reason, also neuromarketing might be considered as a breakthrough in exploring the psychology and behaviour of consumers (Gang *et al.*, 2012). Several authors (such as Lindstrom, 2009; Renvoisé and Morin, 2007) agree that with the help of modern techniques we can directly look into the 'black box' of the body and based on the information received press the 'buy button' in the brain, thus forming effective marketing strategies the human brain cannot resist (Lee *et al.*, 2007).

Despite the technology available today, we can almost certainly say that psychology will not give up questionnaires, tests, and personal interviews. Neuromarketing offers new research tools, but it is not expected that it would completely replace traditional research tools used today (Šebej, 2009).

2.3 Interdisciplinary relations with neuroscience

The term 'neuroscience' is often used regarding neuromarketing, as it is a base for neuromarketing. It is a scientific discipline that aims to understand how the brain and mind function, i.e. to understand the brain processes involved in the perception, cognition, and learning (Kopčo, 2009). Neuroscience examines how the human nervous system works in health and disease, how the nervous system develops throughout life and evolution, explores individual neurons (nerve cells) from the genetic level to the level of neuronal communication, explores different parts of the nervous system and their interconnection, ways of creating hierarchically organized neural networks, their cooperation and relationship to the external behaviour of humans (Beňušková, 2002). As the most important specialized part of neuroscience can be considered:

▸ neuroanatomy: describes the anatomy, morphology, and nervous system;
▸ neurology: deals with clinical implications and pathology of the nervous system;
▸ neuropsychology: focuses on the clinical implications of the nervous system, cognitive aspect, intelligence, and emotions;
▸ neuroendocrinology: studies dealing with the nervous and hormonal system;
▸ cognitive neurosciences: studies about the nervous and cognitive, i.e. identification system.

> Neuroscience is an important discipline of the 20th century. It is addressing particularly studies of the nervous system. Cognitive neuroscience is its application, which studies human cognition, attention, memory, emotions, language, movement, etc. Interdisciplinary relations between neuroscience and cognitive sciences facilitated the trend of combining social sciences and neuroscience. Interdisciplinary sciences such as neuroeconomics, neuromarketing, neuro-decision-making, and neuromanagement are still developing (Ma *et al.*, 2014).

Cognitive neuroscience is a part of neuroscience, which studies what happens in the human brain during cognitive processes such as perception, thinking, learning, memorizing, recalling from memory, etc. (Kvasnička and Clementis, 2005). Cognitive neuroscience seeks to answer the questions regarding the role of different brain structures in various cognitive activities, when processing and storing information. It studies the relationship between the levels of the brain to reveal causal patterns and to explain cognition, i.e. knowledge of man and animals about the world. Neuroscience and cognitive neuroscience are natural sciences, they are thus based mainly on experimental research. New concepts and theories are tested experimentally to be confirmed or refuted (Gáliková, 2013).

The history of the neuroscientific study of behaviour also reflects an interaction between two approaches, in this case a neurobiological approach and physiological approach. In the standard neurological approach of the last century human patients or experimental animals with brain lesions were studied in a range of behavioural tasks. The behavioural deficits of the subjects were then correlated with their neurological injuries and the correlation used to infer function. What marks many of these studies during the classical period neurology is that they often focused on damage to either sensory systems or movement control systems. In contrast to the neurological approach, the physiological approach involves correlating direct measures or biological states, as in the firing of action potentials in neurons, changes in blood flow, and changes in neuro transmitters, with events in the outside world. During the classical period, this more precise set of methodological tools was extremely powerful for elucidating basic features of nervous function but was extremely limited in its applicability to complex mental states. The results were an almost complete restriction of physiological approaches during the classical period to the study of sensory encoding in the nervous system (Glimcher and Fehr, 2014).

> Neuromarketing uses knowledge of neuroscience for a deeper understanding of consumer behaviour. In general we can say that neuroscience methods examine the behaviour of customers in the process of purchasing decision-making (Glimcher *et al.*, 2009), but also contribute to a better understanding of psychological and neurological events and emotions in advertising, consumer competitions, or product placement.
>
> (Reimann, 2011)

Neuromarketing is evolving simultaneously with neuroscience and offers many opportunities for different types of studies. An example is the well-known competition between Coca-Cola and Pepsi. In a study, the respondents compared samples of both said drinks, while their brains were scanned by MRI. Certainly, the volunteers did not know which drink they just tasted, as the study was conducted through a blind test. The questionnaire found that half of them preferred Pepsi and the other half Coca-Cola. However, a result of neurotesting was different. Most respondents preferred Coca-Cola, as their brain showed high activity in the cranial area associated with memory and emotions. In other words, the strength of Coca-Cola is so great that it sets the brain to fall in love with its taste and thus can influence the purchasing decisions in the store (Penenberg, 2011).

2.4 Interdisciplinary relations with neuroeconomy

The birth of neuroeconomy grew from a number of related factors that simultaneously influenced what were basically two separate communities, although communities with significant overlap. A group of behavioural economists and cognitive psychologists looked towards functional brain imaging as a tool to both test and develop alternatives to neoclassical/revealed preference theories (especially when too many theories chase too few data using choices as the only class of data). A group of physiologists and cognitive neuroscientists looked towards economic theory as a tool to test and develop an algorithmic model of the neural hardware for choice (Glimcher and Fehr, 2014).

Vlăsceanu (2014) states that neuroeconomics and neuromarketing are new emerging interdisciplinary fields that offer a new vision of the decision-making process and both are established on various disciplines and have borrowed a number of methods, techniques, and tools of neuroscience. Neuroeconomics is based on e.g. neuroscience, economics, mathematics, statistics, and cognitive sciences, while neuromarketing is based on fields such as neuroscience, economics, and psychology. Neuroeconomics focuses on the activity of our brains when we are in the evaluation process of reward (decision-making process about money) or fear e.g. if we calculate risks. Neumärker (2007) points out that neuroeconomists believe that the study of neural mechanism behind human decision-making process is essential for finding right and unique decision mechanism for the accurate prediction of behaviour and economic outcomes. Neuroeconomics rediscovers the research of the classical contributors to the economic theory of human behaviour by adding and specifying important components of human behaviour (many of which are ignored in standard economics), by arguing on the unity of behavioural sciences and by drawing the economist's attention to the brain processes of human decisions (De Oliveira *et al.*, 2014).

The approach known as neuroeconomics suggested incorporating some ideas and scientific discoveries from psychology, neuroscience, and economic areas, as an attempt to exactly specify models of decision-making in the human mind. Neuroeconomics as a discipline can thus be defined as the application of neuroscience methods, which examine and analyse behaviour that is economically relevant (Kenning and Plassmann, 2005).

Unlike traditional approaches, which try to explain changes by identifying the decision-making mechanisms, neuroeconomics reflects brain activity, by which it can offer results in a higher level of expertise. Most neuroeconomics studies include decision-making tasks (Murawski, 2011).

Gul and Pesendorfer (2008) argue that neuroeconomics is obviously far from economics, because it addresses different questions, uses different abstractions, and deals with different areas of study. According to them, neuroeconomics is relevant only as a source of inspiration for economists. They also claim that the findings of neuroeconomics studies are irrelevant and are not able to help improve the economy.

Aydinonat (2010), on the other hand, argues that findings in neuroeconomics help to deepen knowledge of economists (e.g. about money, monetary illusions, price fluctuation, strategic pricing, etc.) and to improve comprehension.

Neuroeconomics is the science that examines how the brain forms economic decisions. It helps us understand the strategies that people use when making decisions (Houser and McCabe, 2008), especially the brain's ability to process more alternatives to select the optimal option (Barkin, 2013). It has also become important for studying the neurobiological points of economic behaviour, such as for purchasing decision-making (Sacks, 1984).

Neuroeconomics as a scientific discipline challenges the idea that emotions may harm economic decisions. On the contrary, it believes that emotions can attract people's attention and motivate them to focus better on the area of problem-solving. The reason for integrating various disciplines is based on the idea that human behaviour in the financial sector often seems irrational, which corresponds to the fact of how people decide in casinos, bookmakers, or stock markets.

With the prospect of a deeper understanding of the economic man ('homo oeconomicus') neuroeconomics extends the concept of behavioural economics by neuroscience methods and examines the impact of emotions on economic decisions (Fugate, 2007). Its main objective is to construct a model of decision-making that is not limited only to economic thinking, but is more realistic (Kenning and Plassmann, 2005).

2.5 Interdisciplinary relations with neuromanagement

The term 'neuromanagement' was created by Chinese professor Ma in 2006. Its aim is to investigate brain activity when dealing with various management and economic problems. Within neuromanagement cognitive tools of neuroscience are used such as electroencephalography, electromyography, positron emission tomography, functional magnetic resonance imaging, and near infrared spectroscopy (Ma *et al.,* 2012).

Neuromanagement indicates a new perspective of revealing deep mechanisms behind human behaviour and represents a new source of information. Information obtained directly from the human body is more objective and reliable than traditional measurement through questionnaires or interviews (Ma and Wang, 2006).

Simply put, the neuropsychological data are generally not affected by subjective bias, variance, or demand, but provide a reliable source of information (Dimoka *et al.*, 2012).

2.6 Interdisciplinary relations with sensory marketing

For two decades, the merchants in various industries are trying to get closer to consumers through sensory marketing and new research suggests that many other companies will use sensory marketing soon.

Sensory marketing can be defined as a group of key levers which are controlled by the producer and/or by the distributor to create to specific multisensory atmosphere around the product or the service either by focusing on sale outlet environment or product environment, and the communication or characteristics of the product itself (Filser, 2003). Sensory marketing strategies are specifically proposed by product categories: ordinary/common, complex/technological, hedonist/identity where a set of various methodologies are readily available (Giboreau and Body, 2007).

The use of neuroscience is found in sensory marketing based on studies of visual and non-visual responses to light (CIE, 1924).

Aradhna Krishna from the University of Michigan is considered to be the most prominent expert in the field of sensory marketing, with her publication 'Customer Sense: How the 5 Senses Influence Buying Behaviour' from 2013. The primary reasons of the studies were the questions such as: Why wine in wine glasses tastes better than from an ordinary glass for water? Why a dessert looks better if the fork is placed on the right side of the plate? Why the smell of cinnamon heats the human body? Krishna discovered that senses amplify each other. If the sensory marketing is correctly used in practice, consumers do not perceive it as a marketing message, and therefore do not respond in the usual dismissive way (The Science of Sensory Marketing, 2015).

In 80% of cases the purchasing decision is made impulsively and the goal is to use sensory perception, induce a positive shopping experience, and participate in the creation of emotional ties with the point of sale, product or brand. Achieving these objectives can be through all the sensory capabilities of the customer, whether it is the perception by sight, smell, hearing, touch, and possibly taste. The future concept of multisensory neuromarketing or marketing of the five senses is thus introduced to provide the answers which sensory centres of the customer should be stimulated to respond in the desired manner. All these new names only emphasize what is the content of marketing from the beginning and what is given by its focus on the customer and certainly also his emotional and sensory experiencing (Warmbier, 2008).

2.7 The benefits of neuroscience

Consumer surveys can be significantly beneficial for the study of consumer behaviour and marketing. Over the past decades, neuroscience expanded rapidly, not only in the field of neuromarketing, but also in other neuro-areas. Neurosciences can help to evaluate, improve, or expand existing marketing theories more correctly (Plassmann, 2015), they can provide information about implicit processes that are difficult to access by other methods (Prelec, 2013), better understand individual differences and thereby clarify the heterogeneity of consumers (Venkatraman *et al.*, 2012), and may also clarify assumptions concerning future consumer behaviour (Knutson *et al.*, 2007).

In addition to the previously mentioned, neuroscience approach may be applied in product creation. This way it is guaranteed that the product will reflect the real need of the customer.

There are also articles on neuroethics, neuroergonomics, neuropsychoanalysis, neuroeducation, and the many other neurosciences (Trimble, 2007).

2.8 The prospect of neuromarketing

It is expected that neuromarketing will remain and will be developing just as consumers and brands. Consumers might not even see the difference in the presented marketing messages, but these will be sophisticated and created so as to facilitate a specific buying behaviour. Ethical problems related to marketing will always occur to ensure the transparency of the research. Also, a number of campaigns will be created, not for commercial reasons but for emphasising the changing self-destructive behaviour of people. Neuromarketing has the ability to convince people, e.g. to quit smoking. From the campaigns of various organizations we see that words work more efficiently than images (Morin, 2011).

References

American Psychological Association (APA), 2010. Clinical neuropsychology. Available at: http://tinyurl.com/mm5c8ll.

Aydinonat, N.E., 2010. Neuroeconomics: more than inspiration, less than revolution. Journal of Economic Methodology 17(2): 159-169.

Barkin, E., 2013. The prospects and limitations of neuromarketing. Customer Relationship Management 17: 46-50.

Beňušková, Ľ., 2002. Kognitívna neuroveda. In: Rybár, J., Beňušková, Ľ. and Kvasnička, V. (eds.) Kognitívne vedy. Kalligram, Bratislava, Slovak Republic, pp. 47-104.

Breiter, H.C., Block, M., Blood, A.J., Calder, B., Chamberlain, L., Lee, N., Livengood, S., Mulhern, F.J., Raman, K., Schultz, D., Stern, D.B., Viswanathan, V. and Zhang, F.Z., 2015. Redefining neuromarketing as an integrated science of influence. Frontiers in Human Neuroscience 8: 1073.

Cohen, J.D., 2005. The vulcanization of the human brain: a neural perspective on interactions between cognition and emotion. Journal of Economic Perspectives 19(4): 3-24.

Commission Internationale de l'Éclairage (CIE), 1924. Commission Internationale de l'Éclairage Proceedings. In: Rea, M.S. (ed.) The lumen seen in a new light: making distinctions between light, lighting and neuroscience. Lighting Research and Technology 47(3): 259-280.

Dawson, M.E., Schell, A.M. and Filion, D.L., 2000. The electrodermal system. In: Cacioppo, J.T., Tassinary, L.G. and Bernston, G., 2000. Handbook of psychophysiology. Cambridge University Press, Cambridge, UK, pp. 200-223.

De Oliveira, J.H.C., Giraldi, J.D.M.E. and Dos Santos, R.D.O.J., 2014. Opening the 'Black Box' in the consumer's mind: understanding what is neuromarketing. International Journal of Business and Management 9(9): 96-107.

Dimoka, A., Banker, R.D., Benbasat, I., Davis, F.D., Dennis, A.R., Gefen, D., Gupta, A., Ischebeck, A., Kenning, P., Pavlou, P.A., Müller-Putz, G., Riedl, R., Vom Brocke, J. and Weber, B., 2012. On the use of neurophysiological tools in IS research: developing a research agenda for NeuroIS. MIS Quarterly 36(3): 679-702.

Du Plessis, E., 2011. Jak zákazník vnímá značku: nahlédněte s pomocí neurovědy do hlav spotřebitelů. Computer Press, Brno, Czech Republic, 256 pp.

Filser, M., 2003. Le marketing sensoriel: la quête de l'intégration théorique et managériale. Revue Française du Marketing 194(4-5): 5-11.

Fugate, D.L., 2007. Neuromarketing: a layman's look at neuroscience and its potential application to marketing practice. Journal of Consumer Marketing 24(7): 385-394.

Gáliková, S., 2013. Základy kognitívnej neurovedy. FFTU, Trnava, Slovak Republic, 78 pp.

Gang, D.J., Lin, W., Qi, Z. and Yan, L.L., 2012. Neuromarketing: marketing through science. 2012 International Joint Conference on Service Sciences (IJCSS): 285-289.

Genco, S.J., Pohlmann, A.P. and Steidl, P., 2013. Neuromarketing for dummies. John Wiley, Mississauga, Canada, 408 pp.

Giboreau, A. and Body, L., 2007. Le marketing sensoriel: de la stratégie à la mise en oeuvre. Vuibert, Paris, France, 238 pp.

Glimcher, P.W. and Fehr, E., 2014. Neuroeconomics: decision making and the brain. Academic Press, London, UK, 560 pp.

Glimcher, P.W., Camerer, C.F., Fehr, E. and Poldrack, R.A., 2009. Introduction: a brief history of neuroeconomics. In: Glimcher, P.W., Camerer, C.F., Fehr, E. and Poldrack, R.A. (eds.) Neuroeconomics: decision making and the brain. Academic Press, London, UK, pp. 1-12.

Gul, F. and Pesendorfer, W., 2008. The case for mindless economics. In: Caplin, A. and Schotter, A. (eds.) The foundations of positive and normative economics: a handbook. Oxford University Press, New York, NY, USA, pp. 3-39.

Horská, E., Lajdová, Z. and Kapsdorferová, Z., 2015. Bioeconomics, neuroeconomics and neuromarketing: new approaches to customers and businesses. In: Globalization, economic development, and nation character building. Research Institute of Gunadarma University, Depok, Indonesia, pp. 183-187.

Houser, D. and McCabe, K., 2008. Introduction to neuroeconomics. In: Houser, D. and McCabe, K. (eds.) Neuroeconomics – Advances in health economics and health services research, Vol. 20. Emerald Group Publishing Limited, Bingley, UK, pp. 15-21.

Kalat, J.W., 2011. Biological psychology. Wadsworth, Cengage Learning, Belmont, CA, USA, 608 pp.

Kenning, P. and Plassmann, H., 2005. NeuroEconomics: an overview from an economic perspective. 2nd Conference on NeuroEconomics – ConNEcs 2004. Brain Research Bulletin 67(5): 343-354.

Knutson, B., Rick, S., Wimmer, G.E., Prelec, D. and Loewenstein, G., 2007. Neural predictors of purchases. Neuron 53(1): 147-156.

Kopčo, N., 2009. UNV: Úvod do neurovied. Perception and Cognition Laboratory, Insitute of Computer Science, Faculty of Science, Safarik University, Košice, Slovak Republic.

Kvasnička, V. and Clementis, L., 2005. Prednáška: Kognitívna veda. Available at: http://tinyurl.com/msaz6l6.

Lee, N. and Chamberlain, L., 2007. Neuroimaging and psychophysiological measurement in organizational research: an agenda for research in organizational cognitive neuroscience. Annals of the New York Academy of Sciences 1118: 18-42.

Lee, N., Broderick, A.J. and Chamberlain, L., 2007. What is neuromarketing? A discussion and agenda for future research. International Journal of Psychophysiology 63(2): 199-204.

Lindstrom, M., 2009. Nákupologie: Pravda a lži o tom, proč nakupujeme. Computer Press, Brno, Czech Republic, 240 pp.

Ma, Q.G. and Wang, X.Y., 2006. Management world (in Chinese). In: Ma, Q.G., Hu, L.F., Pei, G.X., Ren, P.Y. and Ge, P. (eds.) Applying neuroscience to tourism management: a primary exploration of neurotourism. Applied Mechanics and Materials 670-671: 1637-1640.

Ma, Q.G., Fu, H.J. and Bian, J., 2012. Management world (in Chinese). In: Ma, Q.G., Hu, L.F., Pei, G.X., Ren, P.Y. and Ge, P., 2014. Applying neuroscience to tourism management: a primary exploration of neurotourism. Applied Mechanics and Materials 670-671: 1637-1640.

Ma, Q.G., Hu, L.F., Pei, G.X., Ren, P.Y. and Ge, P., 2014. Applying neuroscience to tourism management: a primary exploration of neurotourism. Applied Mechanics and Materials 670-671: 1637-1640.

Morin, Ch., 2011. Neuromarketing: the new science of consumer behavior. Society 48(2): 131-135.

Murawski, C., 2011. Neuroeconomics: investigating the neurobiology of choice. Australian Economic Review 44(2): 215-224.

Neumärker, B., 2007. Neuroeconomics and the economic logic of behaviour. In: Analyse and Kritik 29/2007, Lucius & Lucius, Stuttgart, Germany, pp. 60-85.

Ohme, R., Reykowska, D., Wiener, D. and Choromanska, A., 2009. Analysis of neurophysiological reactions to advertising stimuli by means of EEG and galvanic skin response measures. Journal of Neuroscience, Psychology, and Economics 2(1): 21-31.

Penenberg, A.L., 2011. NeuroFocus uses neuromarketing to hack your brain. Fast Company, pp. 84-125.

Plassmann, H., Venkatraman, V., Huettel, S. and Yoon, C., 2015. Consumer neuroscience: applications, challenges, and possible solutions. Journal of Marketing Research 52(4): 427-435.

Prelec, D., 2013. What can neuroscience offer to consumer research? Consumer Neuroscience Satellite Symposium, Lausanne, Switzerland.

Pribišová, K., 2007. Neuropsychológia. In: Heretik, A. (ed.) Klinická psychológia. Psychoprof, Nové Zámky, Slovak Republic, pp. 571-617.

Reimann, M., Schilke, O., Weber, B., Neuhaus, C. and Zaichkowsky, J., 2011. Functional magnetic resonance imaging in consumer research: a review and application. Psychology and Marketing 28(6): 608-637.

Renvoisé, P. and Morin, Ch., 2007. Neuromarketing: understanding the 'Buy Buttons' in your customer's brain. SalesBrain, Thomas Nelson, Nashville, TN, USA, 256 pp.

Sacks, O.W., 1984. A leg to stand on. Touchstone, New York, NY, USA, 224 pp.

Šebej, F., 2009. Úžasný nový svet neuromarketingu. Týždeň 2009: 42. Available at: http://tinyurl.com/kyc89p4.

Sharp, C., Monterosso, J. and Montague, P.R., 2012. Neuroeconomics: a bridge for translational research. Biological Psychiatry 72(2): 87-92.

Shiv, B. and Fedorikhin, A., 1999. Heart and mind in conflict: the interplay of affect and cognition in consumer decision making. Journal of Consumer Research 26: 278-292.

Shiv, B., 2007. Emotions, decisions, and the brain. Journal of Consumer Psychology 17(3): 174-178.

Shubin, T., Tabin, C. and Carroll, S., 2009. Deep homology and the origins of evolutionary novelty. Nature 457: 818-823.

Smidts, A., 2002. Kijken in het brein: over de mogelijkheden van neuromarketing. ERIM Inaugural Address Series Research in Management, EIA-12-MKT, 54 pp. Available at: http://repub.eur.nl/pub/308/.

The Science of Sensory Marketing, 2015. Harvard Business Review 93(3): 28-30. Available at: http://tinyurl.com/ju8qspr.

Thompson, J., 2005. They don't just want your money. They want your brain. Available at: http://tinyurl.com/n2xvngg.

Tinbergen, N., 1951. The study of instinct. Oxford University Press, New York, NY, USA, 228 pp.

Trimble, M.R., 2007. The soul in the brain: the cerebral basis of language, art, and belief. Johns Hopkins University Press, Baltimore, MD, USA, 304 pp.

Venkatraman, V., Clithero, J.A., Fitzsimons, G.J. and Huettel, S.A., 2012. New scanner data for brand marketers: how neuroscience can help better understand differences in brand preferences. Journal of Consumer Psychology 22(1): 143-153.

Vlăsceanu, S., 2014. Neuromarketing and evaluation of cognitive and emotional responses of consumers to marketing stimuli. Procedia – Social and Behavioural Sciences 127: 753-757.

Vysekalová, J. et al., 2011. Chování zákazníka: jak odkrýt tajemství černé skříňky. Grada, Prague, Czech Republic, 356 pp.

Warmbier, W., 2008. Der programmierte Kunde: Neuromarketing – Frontalangriff auf unsere Sinne. Econ, Berlin, Germany, 208 pp.

3. Ethical issues of neuromarketing

*M. Petz and R. Haas**

Institute of Marketing & Innovation, University of Natural Resources and Life Sciences Vienna (Universität für Bodenkultur Wien), Feistmantelstr. 4, 1180 Vienna, Austria; rainer.haas@boku.ac.at

Abstract

Neuromarketing also known as consumer neuroscience is explored with an ethical discourse which includes opinions of researchers and practitioners. We look at the broad scope of neuromarketing, before exploring an Ethical Code of Neuromarketing. Afterwards more critical aspects are covered in detail touching upon legal, moral and praxes related to business, engineering ethics and scientific ethics around specific issues. Some neuromarketing techniques are examined to give an idea of the kind of questions that should be asked as part of an ethical assessment of the technology in an analogous way to technology assessment, which tends to focus on a more operational rather than socio-cultural aspects.

Keywords: ethical code of neuromarketing, neurostandards collaboration, privacy, consumer profiles

Learning objectives

After studying this chapter you should be able to:
- Understand and explain the diversity of ethical issues related to neuromarketing
- Understand the ethical code of neuromarketing and consider it in practical marketing

3.1 Some views about neuromarketing

In this chapter we start with selected views about neuromarketing to illustrate the diversity of ethical issues related to it.

> It's clear that emotion plays an important role in the effectiveness of advertising. It's also clear that exciting progress is being made in measuring these emotions. These are still early days for those approaches, as well as for their ability to explain consumer behaviours. The next five years will be a time of great learning.
>
> Horst Stipp, (Murphy, 2011)

> The Neurostandards collaboration is a process. We are in the early stages, but it will be worth it even if we have to go to Neurostandards 7.0 because the learning that is possible will change the way we all think about advertising.
>
> Bob Woodard, (Murphy, 2011)

> The basic problem remains, however, that the Emotiv system is still a black box solution, and more or less impossible to determine how the scales are made. ... And yes, you may call it ad hominem attacks, but in the tradition of science this is how it is. When you speak bullshit, you are called a bullshitter.

> As you can guess, I am not a proponent of black boxing, particularly not in neuromarketing where we should be able to converge on the same solutions. Quite the contrary. I simply do not understand the need for secrecy among neuromarketing companies. The science is already out there, so why make up new scales? It opens up the possibility of cheating, snake oil production and what is less. Think about the strategic blunders that may be made based on erroneous and unscientific hand waving.
>
> Thomas Ramsøy (Ramsøy, 2013)

> We do not believe that Manchurian customers will be marching down department store aisles any time soon, if ever. Consumers aren't disembodied brains milling about the Mall of America. They juggle their pocketbooks and contemplate other items they have recently bought. ... In the end, a cacophony of influences impinge on us at once, some cancelling out others, some combining in novel ways, some emanating from within us, some from the external environment,

and still others generated by advertisers. Our implicit unconscious processes and overt conscious capacities come together to guide us.

(Genco *et al.*, 2013)

Our contention is that neuroscience findings and methods hold the potential for marketing practices that threaten consumers' abilities to follow preferences and dictates according to free will (Greene, 2003) and contradict Rawlsian justice. This context suggests that external constraints on decision making imposed by applications of neural manipulation are possible violations. Transgressions are particularly troublesome when manipulation occurs without explicit awareness, consent, and understanding.

(Wilson *et al.*, 2008)

As First Amendment scholar C. Edwin Baker says, while speech is only one of many activities that can promote individual autonomy, speech does so 'in a particular, humanly acceptable manner, that is, nonviolently and noncoercively.

If pure speech were otherwise – if, for example, it were more like the imperius curse that allowed evil wizards in the Harry Potter novels to exercise total control over their victims, or like the display of the Queen of Diamonds card that similarly transformed a brainwashed soldier into an unwitting and robotic agent in The Manchurian Candidate' – then we could not feel as safe leaving such a powerful instrument of coercion in people's unregulated hands (which are, indeed, not only unregulated, but constitutionally-shielded from regulation)

Mark Blitz (Blitz, 2009)

If neuromarketing techniques are used properly, we'll have better ads, better products, and happier customers. Who wouldn't want a product they liked more or a less boring commercial? Would consumers really be better off if companies annoyed them with ineffective but costly ad campaigns?

Any marketing tool can be 'evil' if the company behind it misuses it. Advertising can be fun and informative; it can also contain false information or misrepresent the product... Neuromarketing is simply another technique that marketers can use to understand their customers and serve them better.

Roger Dooley (Dooley, 2011)

3.2 The broad scope of neuromarketing

Ethics in neuromarketing is partially dependent on where the system boundary is drawn. While what is ethically acceptable should not change between different application cases, it does. The private and public spheres have different standards as to what is acceptable. Similarly, with neuromarketing what may be acceptable in a research or a specialized research therapeutic context may be unacceptable when applied at a public level. When something concerns the public at large there is often an assumed consent, rather than an explicit consent, with impact on a greater number of people. This may be based on the idea of paternalism, the nanny state (Shapiro, 1988), or just a trespass on the commons (Boyle, 2009; Saba Jr., 2001). The ethical discourse in this chapter is confined to people, and takes an anthropocentric viewpoint. Opting out of hearing (e.g. commercial radio playing in shops, street hawkers) and seeing (e.g. billboards, free newspapers on metros, posters in shop windows) and advertisements in public spaces is not an option in most cases.

To go beyond plain speech or word, to visual cues is to approach the field of neuromarketing. Here we do not have the same semantic awareness and regulations to properly control in the way we have developed with other aspects of marketing and communication. We can look at past cases and see 'blunders' and learn from them in designing our marketing strategies to take in 'such variables as the competitive framework, innovation, resourcefulness, the target market, the firm's existing physical and human resources, brand development, potential areas of conflict and cooperation among institutions, and total customer satisfaction' (Michman and Mazze, 1998). But we cannot conceptualize in the same way how a completely new field of applied neuroscience will actually manifest and be perceived. An example is the virtual world SecondLife (secondlife.com), many of those that enter this world want it to be a game and ask 'So what do I have to do?'. It is hard to give them the concept that, just as life is not a game neither is SecondLife (M. Lipiäinen, 2010 personal communication).

The manufacturer or neuromarketer needs to know what they are conveying; and the audience needs to appreciate what they should get from a communication and not something else. Is it obvious it is an advert, not a public information campaign? Magazines often have warnings saying 'advertising feature' to do this. Or is a communication a navigation aid like a warning traffic light? Consumer education, market creation, and information all need to be applied to train the audience how to respond to neuromarketing approaches (Singh, 2005).

Neuromarketing encompasses a wide range of things and touches on many more (Zurawicki, 2010). Some are neuroscience, behavioural economy, neuropsychology, neuroeconomy, marketing and communication. All of these collectively having implications for public policy, pedagogy, doing business and manufacturing (see Chapter 2 (Bercik, 2017) in this volume for more). And thus the respective fields' own ethics should be considered where there is closeness of application.

Ethics give a justification for a judgement to be made against. However, views on ethics vary with some seeing moral relativism (Gowans, 2015) and others global idealism (Brink, 1989). Furthermore, ethical view-points may take on either Bentham's utilitarian viewpoint of what is for the greatest good in aggregate as a community (Burns, 2005) or Sidgwick's ethical egoism (Sidgwick, 1901) in being individually focused. So following any ethics you fancy as an individual scientist, practitioner or student are not enough, as your personal ethics may not be in accordance with international standards nor others' ethics.

Best thus is probably to develop a code and then, via the *praxis* of implementation, a *de facto* standard-setting. There is precedence for this where DIY biology, citizen science and hacker cultures have taken part in critical reflections to evolve "best practices" (Tenetz, 2011). An ethical standard that is commonly agreed re neuromarketing is needed. Such a standard setting is happening as can be seen with the Ethical Code of Neuromarketing.

3.3 Ethical code of neuromarketing

A code has been developed by the Neuromarketing Science and Business Association (NMSBA) (founded 2012) (NMSBA, 2016). It is called 'The NMSBA Code of Ethics for the Application of Neuroscience in Business' (NMSBA, 2013). See Appendix 1 at the end of this chapter for the full code. It is heavily influenced by 'The ICC/ESOMAR International Code on Market and Social Research' (ICC/ESOMAR, 2008). Which covers many of the marketing aspects that neuromarketers may not have a focus on.

ESOMAR (European Society for Opinion and Market Research) has produced global neuroscience guidelines 'to assist clients who wish to integrate the use of neuroscience in their research.' called, '36 Questions to Help Commission Neuroscience Research' (ESOMAR, 2012). ESOMAR, originally a European Society, is now a worldwide organization and no longer only European in scope (ESOMAR, 2016).

The International Chamber of Commerce (ICC) is active in around 180 countries and has 'developed a large array of voluntary rules, guidelines, and codes – sometimes referred to as 'trade tools', which facilitate cross-border transactions and help spread best practice among companies.' They have put some of these together into an 'Advertising and marketing communication practice Consolidated ICC Code' and set up a website around the codes and standards at www.codescentre.com (ICC, 2014).

Collectively these three organizations provide a framework and advice on how to carry out neuromarketing research and practice ethically. A researcher can apply the letter and spirit of these in a food manufacturing situation, consumer research project or development of therapeutic neuromarketing techniques for medical application and know they are acting reasonably in line with international ethical norms.

As the code is voluntary it provides useful guidelines. It becomes the common norm in the absence of other options. Other options do exist such as the norms set by U.S. federally funded and ethically framed (neuro)science. By extension the wider world research community adopts these ethics as part of their subculture (Motycka, 2011; Resnik, 2015). Legislation is needed to give the code teeth and help enforce its provisions. As copyright and patent laws demonstrate (Boyle, 2009) a jurisprudence around neuromarketing law could be (and is being) developed across different jurisdictions to deal with such criticisms as remain.

3.4 Ethical issues affecting neuromarketing

> There is increasing apprehension among consumer groups and policymakers alike that science and technology are advancing far more rapidly and with much greater invasive impact on consumers than the public is able to fully appreciate, and that these advances are occurring across a wide array of techniques for monitoring many aspects of human behaviour.
>
> (Voorhees *et al.*, 2011)

This quote could be applied to many technologies. The effects of technological change and impact have been debated by philosophers such as John Zerzan from an eco-anarchist viewpoint, who reject the progressive aspects on account of the unknown or increasingly known detriments that have manifested with progress (Zerzan, 2005, Zerzan and Carnes, 1991). Historically, the viewpoint that ethics were for someone else to think about, and not for the proponents or practitioners of a technology (engineering ethics) was acceptable (Brown *et al.*, 2009). Today it is not acceptable to abrogate responsibility to managers, lawyers or anyone else and blithely carry on. Those of us that make use of neuromarketing and related techniques in our professional practice should also be self-critical and responsible. We can look upon ourselves as engineers, explorers or artists, practitioners, scientists or students, but should consider the issues (Table 3.1), which are particularly relevant to neuromarketing.

In the following sections we discuss the ethical issues affecting neuromarketing in the order of Table 3.1.

Table 3.1. Ethical issues affecting neuromarketing.

Fair or sharp business	consumer protection, free speech, unfair commercial practices, validity to potential buyers of research / findings, accreditation
Liability for errors	torts and negligence, injury and adverse reaction reporting
Personal integrity rights	informed consent, privacy issues
Consumer profiles	vulnerable groups, targeted groups, individuals vs groups, stereotyping, tragedy of the commons, everyone's a winner!
Data management	unexpected findings protocol, protecting research participants, data cleaning / updating of info collected, noisy data and false positives
Media and representation	the responsible scientist with a media strategy, sub-cultural differences of perspective for managers and scientists, dublin core
Techniques and praxis	single-neuron recording, fMRI, functional magnetic resonance imaging; and QEEG, quantitative electroencephalography

3.4.1 Fair or sharp business

Consumer protection

Capitalist countries work on the assumption of the free market. The free market is an abstract concept which does not truly exist. There are regulations to ensure that monopolies cannot develop, restrictions on patent, and technology propriety, for essential components and requirements for honesty and fair dealing with competitors and customers (Boyle, 2009). One of the aims is that the customer can be fairly encouraged to buy something and not suffer unlawful coercion to buy. Lawful coercion exists, for example: compulsory public liability insurance is applied to companies who wish to use spaces for trading with the public; and third party liability motor insurance is applied to individuals that want to drive vehicles on public roads.

However, there is a fear that:

> As neuromarketing techniques become more sophisticated and arguably more powerful, the industry will likely face increasing resistance from regulators concerned that consumers are being misled into believing they want or need a product they have no use for, or deceived into thinking a purchase arises from their rational choice whereas in fact they are being induced to act based on stimulated subconscious impulse. To regulators, these techniques may cross the line from fair encouragement to unlawful coercion.
>
> (Voorhees *et al.*, 2011)

Could the same be applied to overweight customers, playing on their fears of social ostracism due to obesity? Such fat shaming can provoke depression and further over eating and impede someone from progressing along the path of change to maintaining a new behaviour (Prochaska, 2008). There is a difference between identifying that need, and perhaps arranging a diner in a way that raises anxiety levels and then promotes 'solutions' to feeling anxious. Such sensory marketing approaches could also be used in the fast-food industry to encourage customers to purchase drinks in the same way that salty food might do nowadays. The burger bar décor of McDonald's Corporation has been criticized in the past, with it claims that has been selected to target children (Vidal, 1997). With lighting and neuromarketing scanning techniques combined on the fly a desire to eat more of something could be engineered on a customer by customer basis. Theoretically the customers are only being encouraged, but coercion by peer pressure or if the customer cannot leave, as they are part of a family party could lead to a kind of passive smoking of dining.

Free speech

Connected to this is the idea of corporate personhood and the rights of free speech. What has this got to do with neuromarketing? Initially speech makes you think of the written or spoken word, but 'speech' can be construed to apply to any kind of communication. This might be branding, color combinations, music, poetry and artistic works. It could also be objects and their arrangement and any kind of neuromarketing technique that communicates to a person. For example, we can be made soporific (by lavender) (Cavanaugh, 2013) or alert (by cinnamon and peppermint) (Barker *et al.*, 2003) by scents which is 'noticeable in the functional magnetic resonance scans even when the scent concentration falls below the threshold for conscious perception' (Zurawicki, 2010). Should such a feedback and scanning system in a shop that used this sensory marketing technique be considered a part of speech?

Our current legal paradigms have worked on 'the idea that rational consideration is the norm for consumer decision making, and nonconscious influence is the exception. But modern brain science tells us just the opposite: Nonconscious influence is the norm and rational consideration is the exception' (Genco *et al.*, 2013). This can be reduced to the debate over free will, and how much free will we really have in the face of propaganda, the onslaught of advertising or peer pressure shaped by those forces. This question of 'autonomy' which is the ability to make and do things of your own volition, and the rights for a corporate person, or anyone else to influence it when it is commercial speech is strongly debated (Blitz, 2009). Viewpoints vary between banning the dangerous art of neuromarketing; as the parliament in France did with a 2011 law stating "Brain-imaging methods can be used only for medical or scientific research purposes or in the context of court expertise" (Oullier, 2012); to a more libertarian pro-capitalist position that 'this kind of regulatory reaction is inappropriate, because it replaces marketplace decision making with legislative decision making' (Genco *et al.*, 2013).

Unfair commercial practices

We have so far talked about passive application of the technology, but it could also be applied aggressively to attack or disparage a rival. Strong negative associations, against a competitor might be found out during investigations and then subtly linked in an advertising campaign to reinforce a negative stereotype. For example, confusion marketing against a brand of crisps, if directly naming the crisps could be banned, but by association may not. Packaging color and design may indicate certain features to consumers. It has been found that:

> Certain correspondences are consistent across culture, whereas others vary... those associations corresponding to natural pairings in the environment such as 'tomato' with red and 'cucumber' with green can be found across countries, whereas other more complex flavours such as 'salt and vinegar' or unspecified flavours such as 'natural' or 'original', tend to have different colour associations depending on the country. These latter associations may only be consistent in those countries in which they exist and have been learned, or internalized, by the consumer.
>
> (Velasco *et al.*, 2014)

There are many cases of associating with the form and packaging design of products that play on such confusion where trademark infringement and copycat packaging has been used to appear as if from a different manufacturer (Marsh, 1996).

Further misleading might happen with lies of omission or lies of commission. Is it ethical to deliberately miss something out a consumer might want to know? If an ingredient is habit forming, as caffeine is, should they be informed about that aspect? If a serving method makes a product feel good, above and beyond its inherent product properties, is it just nice presentation and thus acceptable or a lie? Ready meals / TV Dinners have suffered a lot of criticism for their high fat, high salt content and nutritional quality (NHS Choices, 2015). If a technique was used that made the food taste better than it really was, it could encourage malnutrition, with the impression it was good eating, whereas in fact it was a meal deficient in essential components. Such 'product-extrinsic food cues' are being used to 'influence ... sensory perception, hedonic appraisal, and intake/consumption' (Piqueras-Fiszman and Spence, 2015).

Manipulation to make a consumer not consider these factors would be a lie of omission. Label design can elegantly do this, and manufacturers strive at 'an operation dubbed 'clean label' with the goal of removing the most glaring industrial ingredients and additives from labels' already (Blythman, 2015). How ethical would it be if optical illusions, like moving pictures technology, was applied to a product placement as part of the marketing mix so a consumer did not notice something was absent, which they normally relied upon for decision making? For example, the UK has a traffic light scheme for labelling pre-packaged foods on their fat and salt content, clever design could minimize the impact of that design. It could even promote a manufacturer perspective on a product, such unrealistic portion sizes (NHS Choices, 2015). Manipulation to make a consumers feel they had been adequately fed, when they had not, would be a lie of commission. Spices in food makes this a common manipulation already, so why not use modern technology to do the same? If the formulation of the food is good what's wrong with the idea of persuading someone to eat it?

Playing on common tropes and facilitating or playing off cognitive dissonance could be enabled by neuromarketing. Popular misconceptions, or common confabulations (Schnider *et al.*, 1996) such as the Mandela effect, which was a false memory of Mandela's death shared by many people (Spool, 2015), could be used in elegant ways of subliminally marketing with one product idea and then later playing off by association on another. For example, cupcakes have a positive association for some, and as a result, cupcake shoes and other products sell well by playing off this positivity. Yet for others the association is not there and subliminal emotional marketing passes them by.

> As much as some marketers joke about linking interactive ads directly to consumers' nervous systems to minimize all the guess work and wasted marketing expense, neuroimaging offers a serious foundation to target and connect emotion mining with consumers.
>
> (DeBiase, 2010)

Such emotion mining could develop brand caché by extending a cross media franchise via cross-branding in a food product. Star Wars Coco Pops, a breakfast cereal sold in England in 2015, played upon the positive feelings towards the film franchise in such a way. The Pirates of the Caribbean film series (Jowitt and Oakley-Brown, 2011); which is also popular, but lacking the same cultural resonance (Brooker, 2002), would not be able to do this, and the risk would be avoided, yet with neuromarketing the emotional aspects might be visible enough to be viable and detectable. Would it be ethical to excavate and then exploit consumer minds in this way?

These aforementioned examples refer to a *mens rea* (a guilty mind to intentionally do wrong) to actually do this. The EU law already has provisions that deal with even the use of neuromarketing techniques *per se*.

> The EU's Unfair Commercial Practices Directive prohibits 'unfair commercial practices', which [are]... practices that are 'misleading' and practices that are 'aggressive'... Under the U.K.'s implementation of the Directive,... a commercial practice may be 'misleading' if it omits material information so as to cause the average consumer to purchase a product that he or she would not have otherwise purchased. ...this could be construed to cover an advertiser's failure to disclose its use of neuromarketing techniques, rendering a consumer unable to consider and combat the effect of those techniques on her decision to purchase a product. A practice may be 'aggressive' if it applies 'coercion' or 'undue influence' to impair the average consumer's freedom of choice to purchase a product... Neuromarketing's potential incursions into a consumer's unconscious decision making processes and arguable undermining of free will could fall within the prohibition on 'aggressive' advertising.
>
> (Voorhees *et al.*, 2011)

Validity to potential buyers of research / findings, accreditation

Validity arises partially from standard setting, and thus ease of understanding what is being found out, and its applicability without needing complex translation between practitioners. However, a short cut to this is to have accreditation (Genco *et al.*, 2013). Accreditation can be done for individuals, being accredited to a Self-Funding Regulatory Authority (SEFRA), government agency or a trade association. The ethical question arises more over if the standards are comprehensive enough or omit crucial features for the results to be useful. The pharmaceutical industry with its high expenditures, important life-saving purposes and well educated experimental designers has many examples of drug trials that fail due to poor experimental design (Retzios, 2009). This implies that there is a high probability that neuromarketing without such high budgets, less experienced experimental designers, less life-saving importance and shorter history of setting protocols for praxis is equally if not more prone to failures. Is it ethical to proceed with neuromarketing before these factors are adequately dealt with?

3.4.2 Liability for errors

Torts and negligence

A tort in criminal law or a delict in civil law is where either by action or by inaction someone suffers an injury of some kind and someone is morally responsible for that. Inaction, when institutionally (the company or organization) should have known due to their professionalism or license to carry on that trade or pre-empted a tort by procedure would be negligence. Personal responsibility is also a factor in assessing liability. Vorhees *et al.* highlighted that 'Tort Issues' (The use of neuromarketing techniques to induce purchase of a product which, if misused, could cause personal injury) raises important questions under the law of products liability (Voorhees *et al.*, 2011). So who would be morally responsible? An individual and, do they have professional indemnity insurance? A company that applies a technique in good faith? Or the vendor that sold a solution?

> It is not at all difficult to imagine product liability claims being asserted, especially by or on behalf of children and other vulnerable groups, that neuromarketing wrongfully induced the claimants to use products that are unreasonably dangerous for them, or to over-consume or become dependent on unhealthy foods or beverages, by overriding their rational powers of self-control.
>
> (Voorhees *et al.*, 2011)

Perhaps in this case provision should be made for such claims in the future, perhaps by a consortium of manufacturers or at least by insurers?

Injury and adverse reaction reporting

> Other tort claims may be advanced under a theory that by penetrating to internal areas of brain function, neuromarketing impermissibly 'touches' a protected personal domain giving rise to liability for battery or assault.
>
> (Voorhees *et al.*, 2011)

This is tricky to answer ethically, who can operate full body scanners? Who can carry out intimate procedures? Which procedures and when can they carry them out? This is a big ethical issue as mass introduction of any technique does mean that there will be people that refuse to consent to it and there is a high probability that for some it will be harmful. Just as there is no safe food and no safe medicine for everyone it must be questioned if any neuromarketing technique won't also find its share of affected peoples who suffer some level of injury.

Allergies have been claimed for water (aquagenic urticarial) and electricity (electrical sensitivity) and it is likely that some will claim similar for neuromarketing techniques if they become widespread. It is prudent to seek a protocol with how such perceptions can be reported by a purported sufferer (real, vexatious or wrongly attributed) and dealt with properly. Perhaps the Yellow Card Scheme, which makes use of citizen science, is a possibility (MHRA, 2016)? It could be implemented by use of Quick Response Codes (QR codes) put on equipment and places where neuromarketing is applied, and if linked in with mobile apps and an electronic reporting system could be rolled out internationally, much as happens with EudraVigilance which is 'a data processing network and management system for reporting and evaluating suspected adverse drug reactions (ADRs)' (EMA, 2015).

3.4.3 Personal integrity rights

Informed consent

Consent can be given:

Explicitly by writing and filling out paperwork. It can be attached to a document outlining the rights of withdrawal of data and consent at any time. There can be an advocate for the person who consents, that is able to understand for them the implications of what is consented to and make considered recommendations. This is the ideal in a research context.

Implicitly by making it obvious through signage and common norms that entering this website, store, mall or manufacturing environment gives consent. Here making sure that people know, understand and agree is harder. Stupid people or some vulnerable groups can find it hard to consent to what a reasonable person can actually consent to. Here consent may be presumed by society on their behalf (society accepts everyone can be exposed if in a common space) or they have guardians or others that look out for their interests. Ratings systems and licenses can be given if it is felt age or other restrictions on access are required.

Privacy issues

The right to privacy is a difficult concept to understand for those that never had privacy. There has 'been a shift towards greater openness' Professor Gavin Phillipson claims and that 'young people growing up with social media [are being] ... taught that the important thing is to express yourself, ... which indicates a kind of shift away from the notion of privacy and individual dignity' (Phillipson, 2013). Yet throughout the EU we now have a personal privacy right to our private and family life, our home and our correspondence (Phillipson, 2013). By moral extension that extends to thoughts and communications in a privacy sphere.

'...claims by neuromarketers about the power of their techniques to understand brain function and impact behavior have predictably raised privacy concerns among regulators and the general public' (Voorhees *et al.*, 2011). The right to privacy is needed for the mentally well-functioning of people.

> And that's for a number of reasons: the development of intellectual faculties through reading, through private conversation, through writing privately, for example keeping a diary; the right to form intimate relationships – sexual relationships are obviously physically carried on in private spaces, without anyone else watching, but generally it's thought that intimate human relationships need privacy to flourish, and similarly with family life.
>
> (Phillipson, 2013)

3.4.4 Consumer profiles

Vulnerable groups

Any individual may have a weakness. When a group of people have features in common it can be called a cohort. Members of a cohort may share a number of weaknesses which makes them then vulnerable to perhaps manipulation or side-effects of a technique applied to them. Even within a vulnerable cohort there may be some for whom there is even greater vulnerability, for example children with learning difficulties or psychological conditions compared with normal children. This makes some more 'weak and vulnerable'.

The 'weak and vulnerable' consumer was considered when drafting the EU Unfair Commercial Practices Directive and although this was not adopted as the 'generally applicable standard. ...When commercial practices are likely to materially distort the economic behaviour of only a clearly identifiable group of consumers who, for various reasons, are particularly vulnerable to the practice or the underlying product in a way that the trader could reasonably expect to foresee, then the practices must be assessed from the perspective of the average member of that vulnerable group' (DG Justice, 2015).

The directive goes on to directly say that 'vulnerable consumers are those more exposed to a commercial practice or a product because of their (1) mental or physical infirmity, (2) age or (3) credulity' and then expands this saying it may 'cover a wide range of situations' (DG Justice, 2015).

Targeted groups

It is a common marketing technique to identify a target market of a profiled group of consumers rather than undifferentiated mass-marketing approach. Such segmentation may be done on psychographic, cultural, behavioural, community of interest or other grounds alone or in combination. Segmentation may be quite broad with men, women, children, retired, but for niche marketing could be focused to look at personality differences, ethnic or cultural awareness, geographical origin as well as income levels and prior spending habits. Research in neuromarketing has begun to validate some of these categories (Zurawicki, 2010).

Already the Federal Trade Commission in the USA has stated that 'protecting children from unfair and deceptive advertising is a priority for the agency, noting that 'children may be deceived by an image or a message that likely would not deceive an adult' (Voorhees *et al.*, 2011). Other market segments that regulators have investigated include 'the elderly and members of minority groups based on similar concerns about these groups' vulnerability to advertising claims' (Voorhees *et al.*, 2011).

Individuals versus groups

Often with data collection, the concept of 'metadata' is mentioned. The simple definition is that, this is data about data, and does not reveal much. However, a better understanding is gained by realising that:

> Taken alone, pieces of metadata may not seem to be of much consequence. However, technological advancements mean that metadata can be analysed, mined and combined in ways that make it incredibly revelatory. When accessed and analysed, metadata can create a comprehensive profile of a person's life – where they are at all times, with whom they talk and for how long, their interests, medical conditions, political and religious viewpoints, and shopping habits.
>
> (Privacy International, 2016)

> This is quite significant as 'the former head of the CIA, Michael Hayden, remarked in 2014: 'We kill people based on metadata'
>
> (Privacy International, 2016)

Legally much metadata may be freely used, stored and processed. This is fast changing and the law is unclear, with arguments made for some being personal data (and not free for use) and some that once it has been disclosed to a service provider it loses that personal status and thus restrictions (Kamara, 2014; Voin, 2015). Better data segregation of metadata would protect customers and firms and prepare better for future changes. With neuromarketing there could be more forms of metadata that are useful, for example the times of day a research subject is not so aware and capable of rationally making a purchase decision. This is how metadata can be useful from one individual, but data can be collected in aggregate, which brings new moral questions.

While aggregate data is collated by individuals, and individuals must have worked together to create the profiles and write the software, etc. it is often done in a way that makes it impossible to assign specific holistic responsibility to one researcher. An example of this is Google Analytics (www.google.com/analytics) that can be used as a tool by a business for gaining and marketing insights from users of websites. Perhaps even direct marketing to individual users, who will all vary having 'individualized cognitive brain structures and performance levels' (Zurawicki, 2010). While at present, neuromarketing experts may scoff at Google Analytics having this capability, ubiquitous computing and the development of virtual reality headsets like the Rift (www.oculus.com/en-us/rift/) may move in the direction that eye tracking and other physiological data gained while in a virtual world can be used in this way (Greenfield, 2006). Who would be liable should there be an unforeseen issue from that personally targeted marketing? Alphabet Inc.? Oculus VR LLC? The business exploiting Google's data or a combination? We have two issues here:

Issue 1: stereotyping

The stereotyping and resultant action individuals suffer as being linked, perhaps falsely linked, is correctly termed group attribution error which is related to the fundamental attribution error. It is one of a number of cognitive biases that may arise from researchers being human, computer programming being done by humans and a combination of the two. Like logical fallacies, these are not *per se* neuromarketing ethical issues, but the praxis of consumer neuroscience may make them relevant. Training and awareness can help to mitigate this danger. In fact, it has been claimed that 'Neuroscience methods generally avoid cognitive biases like social desirability that are difficult for traditional methods' (Genco *et al.*, 2013).

If so then ethically such neuromarketing methods should be used alongside traditional methods to help weed out those biases. It would be unethical not to use them. Social desirability bias is when people under report undesirable behaviour (e.g. how often they eat sweets) and over report desirable behaviour (e.g. how often they drink water rather than sugary drinks) suggests itself as such an application case. However, the current state of the art and praxis approaches the pseudoscience of lie detector tests, which are not reliable.

Issue 2: tragedy of the commons

The tragedy of the commons, whereby all with an interest in gathering data take that data, yet none take responsibility for the transgressions that result. The software engineer who made the tools, the researcher that shaped the protocol, the businesses that benefited from the findings are not easily identifiable and cannot be identified at the individual and sometimes even the organizational level. Everyone is guilty but no-one is liable. Here negligence, rather than malfeanse, misfeance or willful nonfeanse is more likely. Illustrated thus:

> A company hires a catering company to provide drinks and food for a retirement party. If the catering company doesn't show up, it's considered nonfeasance. If the catering company shows up but only provides drinks (and not the food, which was also paid for), it's considered misfeasance. If the catering company accepts a bribe from its client's competitor to undercook the meat, thereby giving those present food poisoning, it's considered malfeasance.
> (Wikipedia, 2016)

Effectively any burden is born by the society at large. However, any benefits will also be borne by the society at large. Ethically the precautionary principle is not being followed here and perhaps it should? The data is being treated as a commons, which can be enclosed or mined to make a profit from it (Boyle, 2009). Such exploitation is effectively taking value from others with perhaps scant reward and even carrying out actions the individuals taken from do not want.

Everyone's a winner

Ethically neuromarketing may also offer benefits at the group level, in respect to public policy implications. Practical moral philosophy, which is what ethics is, includes hedonistic or happiness ethics. Michel Onfray's *Contre-histoire de la philosophie* book series explores this through history (Ireland, 2006). It can be ethical to carry out a course of action, rather than refrain from one. Public service is one such example of this. It has been claimed that:

> public service advertising (PSA), public policy design, and education' are 'three areas where neuromarketing [can] be a source of good in society' (Genco et al., 2013). 'PSAs that are meant to change long term behavior – such as

> promoting smoking cessation, immunization, medical checkups… [find that]
> – emotions are perhaps even more important…[than] traditional ads, which
> usually evoke only the positive end of the emotional spectrum, PSAs tend to
> use a much wider emotional palette…. evoking negative emotions – disgust,
> anger, even fear – with an assertive message about how to overcome those
> emotions, can be a powerful motivator of action or behavioural change.
>
> (Genco *et al.*, 2013)

The scope for such social marketing's (Kotler and Zaltman, 1971) application in the food industry: for instance, to encourage the five fruits a day; avoid products deleterious to health like fried chicken suppers or even to motivate long term dietary change in a target cohort is appealing. Smoking cessation offers the strongest evidence for neuromarketing being successful in long-term behavioural change (Falk *et al.*, 2011), but perhaps appeals to emotion only work on the kinds of people that smoke and needed smoking cessation therapy? Or the ones that were successful? Extrapolation, with such lack of clarity has ethical implications, despite the appealing nature of the research, a hasty conclusion could arise from several logical fallacies and poor statistical techniques.

Public policy design is a more successful and clearer example where neuromarketing could be successful (Genco *et al.*, 2013). Policy interventions are commonly tailored for a target cohort. An example is, encouragement to eat more iron containing food in the diet of first trimester pregnant women. Here design of choice architecture can create defaults and 'nudge' behaviour in that direction (Sunstein and Thaler, 2012). Given the limited time for change this can be easily measured and neuromarketing research can identify where and perhaps why certain hard to reach individuals are not nudged. Ethical questions remain about if people should be nudged to adopt a certain behaviour, which later on may prove to be harmful, but from a public policy point of view, it is better to design programs and interventions to be effective rather than money wasters.

Neuromarketing research and techniques for education is so broad that for sure a positive impact can be made. Analysis of memory and learning can show which memory is being used and thus very important aspects can be seen to be wanted as long term or not. Age specific memories might be strengthened for short term or long term via neuroscience techniques such as altering the mood and assessing affect in a subject during an episode of memory formation, encoding or recall (Zurawicki, 2010). Memories could be widely implanted. Here the biggest ethical questions relate to the purpose of education and are not really neuromarketing questions at all.

3.4.5 Data management

Unexpected findings protocol

Some of the techniques that are being applied in consumer neuroscience reveal anomalies that indicate a pathology may be present or may be developing. Developing a protocol for such unexpected findings is the ethically correct response. With medicine, a triage system has evolved (Green-Yellow-Red-Black) that neuroscience and neuromarketers can well adapt aspects of to health related findings of concern. This could range from doing nothing and not informing the research participant (Green), as some physiological conditions are irregular, but fairly common so little can be done about them; to counselling and treatment with a physician (Red). Ethically who should bear the costs (a researcher organization or public health care or the person's own insurance) has been explored (Emanuel *et al.*, 2004) in respect to health research on a population, and the same can be applied in neuroscience cases.

A protocol that research subjects and researchers are aware of and both commit to allows questions of a medical-legal, bioethical, medical ethics, engineering ethics, business ethics, and financial implications to be satisfactorily combined. This protocol should be agreed to before any research begins. It is morally acceptable to insist that a participant consents to being informed of any negative findings or otherwise refusing to use them in research. Similarly, action must be taken if someone is found to pose a risk to others, e.g. an air traffic controller showing signs of sleep apnoea. To not do that would be medically negligent.

Protecting research participants

Research participants need their data protecting from large corporations, the state and insurers who may use it. Protection can come from following a protocol for unexpected findings, but also a data management policy. Such a policy also includes confidentiality and informing a research participant about the needs for this. When research goes beyond investigation to innovation development and implementation then old data may need reappraising and perhaps even original research participants reinvestigating. Proper record keeping can allow anonymization of data, but still allow back tracing if so needed. At least in theory.

Data cleaning / updating of info collected

Any data that is collected will need cleaning. Raw data should only be accessible to the original research team. The interpretation and any data that is passed on from that corpus can then be controlled and contextualized. It can also be cleaned. Data cleaning can have two meanings that are paradoxical in ethical terms.

1. It can mean removing anomalies, outliers, smoothing curves and accentuating findings to support a certain position. When this is done as cherry picking, it is a logical fallacy to rely on that cherry picked data for conclusions and ethically unacceptable.

2. The other form of cleaning is desirable. It is when data was collected a while ago and the details have changed, maybe closer scrutiny reveals more accurate interpretations. For example, a participant moves address or changes name, perhaps after marriage. A change in medicine or diet of a research participant may also affect physiological and concomitant health aspects. Here cleaning of the data means that a database that generates reports uses the cleaned aspects in generating the reports and not just the original collected data.

The original data should always be kept in its original form, as computer manipulation and data transference can cause data loss and data corruption. Even automated processes that have no room for human error do this.

Noisy data and false positives

With any collection of data of a natural science nature it will be noisy. With any data there will be false positives. A good awareness of statistics, can help to read and interpret this data with a professional viewpoint. Proper technology assessment and outside supervision, with review boards, auditing and wide consultation help reduce the impact of noise and false positives on the relatively new field of neuromarketing.

3.4.6 Media and representation

The responsible scientist with a media strategy

Anyone communicating about neuroscience is counselled to take advice and training from those more expert in communication: press officers, peers that have experience of successful communications or even friendly journalists. Refusing to give a quote by saying 'no comment', planned press releases and press conferences are good tactics to gain time for prepared media interactions. Gaining copy approval, press embargoes and limited releases are ways to control the media. Ideally, where appropriate a media strategy should be developed around a project that includes what can be said, by who and when and to who. Thus client confidentiality, participant protection and effective marketing can be planned for. It may be that publishing information is required. Grant funders, professional funders, financial regulations, educator criteria for course completion or professional development can all have their own requirements. Some of these demand exclusivity and peer review. Planning for these and what is permitted and required is important too.

Specifically:

> ...neuromarketers have an obligation to maintain scientific transparency in media and marketing communications that goes beyond what is required of traditional market research providers, because their methods are so new and different and many of the underlying scientific principles are so counterintuitive.
>
> (Genco *et al.*, 2013)

Sub-cultural differences of perspective for managers and scientists

How can you be a responsible scientist when there is pressure to deliver a result? When data is ambiguous? There can be commercial pressures, which impinge on having enough data. Ethically caveats should be given about what data says and what it does not say. Non-scientists often want a clear unambiguous statement of fact. Sometimes it is not possible to give this. Scottish law has three verdicts: guilty, not guilty and not proven. When asked for findings the not proven finding is a valid finding (Samuel, 2005). It can be supplemented, by expert opinion and impressions of a trend in data or findings which are more to the liking of a client, only if these are properly contextualized. It is better not to include statements that can be quoted out of context or say nothing than give a wrong-headed thinker support in their mistaken views.

Different cultures (e.g. research scientists, marketers, manufacturers) expect different ways of presenting and have different responses to information. Business managers are results orientated and want to have the information to make a decision. A non-decision is often not an option they want. Awareness of this, allows data confidence levels to be given, so that they still can make a decision, but know how un/reliable it is. Ideally, validation should be given both internally and externally:

> Internal and external validity: At a minimum, internal validity checks must be based on a sufficiently comprehensive research database to provide meaningful and effective results to neuromarketing consumers. Ensuring external and sustained validity requires neuromarketers to align their products and

metrics with changing technologies and expanding neuroscience knowledge. Maintenance of safety and efficacy verification in neuromarketing research, development, and deployment is absolutely required.

(Murphy *et al.*, 2008)

A dialog between researchers and users of their findings can help to translate information via usability engineering so it is relevant and useful to different parties. Vendors of neuromarketing solutions may be the best people to do this (Genco *et al.*, 2013). Here ethical aspects are commonly conflated with quality assurance ones. Here muddled thinking, conflation and lack of clarity may make it unclear between what is good practice and what is ethical practice (Airaksienen, 1998). Truth is not an ethic, telling the truth is an ethical practice, if it is a good or a bad ethical practice depends on your personal morals and the purpose it is put to. Confidentiality on pricing between B2B clients is prudent to maintain market share, but it is not an ethical decision to make it open or not.

Dublin Core

Murphy *et al.*'s (2008) 'comprehensive research database' can be gained by using previously published research. There are solutions that allow access based on levels of restriction and permission. Data can be appropriately classified by using the Dublin Core Schema that labels information and artifacts, which are called objects in the Dublin Core (DC) terminology, in whatever form it has with meta-data tags. Tags are comprehensive, called DCMI Metadata Terms and are explained on the DC website (dublincore.org/documents/dcmi-terms). However, a big ethical question remains about how long that data can be kept and who can access it. Article 6, section d. of the NMSBA Code of Ethics states:

Personal information collected shall be collected for specified Neuromarketing research purposes and not used for any other purpose.'

And 6g:

'The Neuromarketing research data itself, including brain scans and brain data shall remain the property of the research company and will not be shared. (see Appendix A for the code).

Which makes it hard to see how validation can occur if the code is followed. And for those lacking a database already, if they cannot acquire it from reputable sources they might fall back on using other ways that are less reliable to get data such with the program DataThief (datathief.org).

Awareness of new techniques and changes in the field come from keeping up with research findings in the scientific literature and being aware of changes. This is best done by academics and those that are using neuromarketing techniques are well advised to make use of the concept of the triple or even quintuple helix (Leydesdorff, 2012) and ensure that they have a suitable academic partner involved in their project team.

3.4.7 Techniques and praxis

For best results techniques are often used in combination with each other or with other techniques such as eye tracking and more traditional market research methods like interviews, questionnaires or focus groups. Technical advances in neuroscience should result in models which 'will prove more robust to new situations and contexts' (Plassmann *et al.*, 2015). Ethical questions will arise over each technique that are peculiar to it or its relationship to other techniques which it may be used concert with.

Single-neuron recording

Single-neuron recording has been mostly done on monkeys and some on rats with implications for foraging, creativity and learning (Shadlen and Kiani, 2013). It has been extended to people undergoing some surgical treatments for pharmacologically intractable epilepsy which 'require placing electrodes, either as probes fairly deeply within the brain or as a grid on the surface of the cortex' (Rey *et al.*, 2014). This limits the research as 'ethical standards prohibit implanting probes in healthy human brains; the number of probes used, and thus the number of neurons identified, is limited to the number medically required' (Cerf *et al.*, 2015). It is the invasive nature of the procedure that makes it ethically unacceptable for mere marketing research. We accept implants and cyborgs when it comes to art so why not allow those that want to, to participate in invasive research?

fMRI – functional magnetic resonance imaging

Functional magnetic resonance imaging (fMRI) has been criticized on the basis that:

> The MRI machine is not the most natural environment; it is uncomfortable ...
> and very noisy ...exceed 90 dB. Evidence exists that such adverse environmental
> characteristics may have a substantial (negative) impact on cognition and
> choice (Arnsten and Goldman-Rakic, 1998; Jacob *et al.*, 2015), thus potentially
> distorting any relationship between brain and (population behavior).
> (Boksem and Smidts, 2015)

Not only does this make the marketing research conclusions questionable, but there are health implications to be considered when deciding if it is appropriate to use. These include DNA damage which may promote cancer (Knuuti *et al.*, 2013), heating of internal body tissues and magnetic effects, which are considered largely benign. Though over exposure is possible, if too long or too powerful a magnetic force is applied (Hartwig *et al.*, 2009). The precautionary principle would err away from any use.

Quantitative electroencephalography

This technique has few if any risks. Risks would be allergic reactions to metal, saline or gels for connecting to the body. However, the praxis of the technology requires consideration of some risk.

In rare instances, an electroencephalography can cause seizures in a person with a seizure disorder. This is due to the flashing lights or the deep breathing that may be involved during the test (Health Library, 2016).

Ethically there are not questions over the technology but rather the findings and usefulness of what can be a lengthy preparation of a subject, compared with other tests; and a test which in the end may not identify a region of the brain as precisely as some other test, such as single-neuron recording.

Similar analysis can be applied to other techniques that may be considered, which looks at the detriments and benefits and weighs them appropriately. Likewise, ethical questions can be explored with the pros and cons of different positions and perspectives via the literature, expert opinion and allied fields to consumer neuroscience. By this method an ethical position can be taken and defended as needed.

References

Airaksienen, T., 1998. Professionalism and science. In: Lewicka-Strzałecka, A. and Loukola, O. (eds.) Science in society 2: science policy and ethics. University of Helsinki. IfiS Publishers, Warsaw, Poland, pp. 43-49.

Arnsten, A.F. and Goldman-Rakic, P.S., 1998. Noise stress impairs prefrontal cortical cognitive function in monkeys: evidence for a hyperdopaminergic mechanism. Archives of General Psychiatry 55: 362-368.

Barker, S., Grayhem, P., Koon, J., Perkins, J., Whalen, A. and Raudenbush, B., 2003. Improved performance on clerical tasks associated with administration of peppermint odor. Perceptual and Motor Skills 97: 1007-1010.

Berčík, J., 2017. Interdisciplinary relations of neuromarketing and neuropsychology. Chapter 2. In: Horská, E. and Berčík, J. (eds.) Neuromarketing in food retailing. Wageningen Academic Publishers, Wageningen, the Netherlands, pp. 37-48.

Blitz, M., 2009. Neuromarketing, subliminal messages, and freedom of speech. Neuroethics and Law Blog: An interdisciplinary forum for legal and ethical issues related to the mind and brain. Available at: http://tinyurl.com/o7dk9r.

Blythman, J., 2015. Swallow this: serving up the food industry's darkest secrets. HarperCollins Publishers, New York, NY, USA, 320 pp.

Boksem, M A. and Smidts, A., 2015. Brain responses to movie trailers predict individual preferences for movies and their population-wide commercial success. Journal of Marketing Research 52: 482-492.

Boyle, J., 2009. The public domain: enclosing the commons of the mind. University Press of Florida, Gainesville, FL, USA, 672 pp.

Brink, D.O., 1989. Moral realism and the foundations of ethics. Cambridge University Press, Cambridge, UK, 340 pp.

Brooker, W., 2002. Using the force: creativity, community and star wars fans. Bloomsbury Academic, London, UK, 254 pp.

Brown, J.K., Lee Downey, G. and Diogo, M.P., 2009. The normativities of engineers: engineering education and history of technology. Technology and Culture 50: 737-752.

Burns, J.H., 2005. Happiness and utility: Jeremy Bentham's equation. Utilitas 17: 46-61.

Cavanaugh, J.L., 2013. Examining the differential effects of natural and synthetic aromas of lavender and peppermint on cognition, mood, and subjective workload. PhD thesis, University of Colorado, Denver, CO, USA.

Cerf, M., Greenleaf, E., Meyvis, T. and Morwitz, V.G., 2015. Using single-neuron recording in marketing: opportunities, challenges, and an application to fear enhancement in communications. Journal of Marketing Research 52: 530-545.

Debiase, D.A., 2010. Preface. In: Zurawicki, L. (ed.) Neuromarketing: exploring the brain of the consumer. Springer-Verlag, Berlin, Germany, 273 pp.

DG Justice, 2015. Anon. Unfair commercial practices European Commission > UCP > guidance. Directorate-General Justice and Consumers, European Commission, Brussels, Belgium. Available at: http://tinyurl.com/lzt9sfn.

Dooley, R., 2011. Brainfluence: 100 ways to persuade and convince consumers with neuromarketing. John Wiley and Sons, New York, NY, USA, 304 pp.

Emanuel, E.J., Wendler, D., Killen, J. and Grady, C., 2004. What makes clinical research in developing countries ethical? The benchmarks of ethical research. Journal of Infectious Diseases 189: 930-937.

ESOMAR, 2012. ESOMAR launches global neuroscience guidelines. ESOMAR, Amsterdam, the Netherlands.

ESOMAR, 2016. About ESOMAR. Available at: http://tinyurl.com/krgdkye.

European Medicines Agency (EMA), 2015. Mandatory e-reporting essentials. EMA, London, UK.

Falk, E.B., Berkman, E.T., Whalen, D. and Lieberman, M.D., 2011. Neural activity during health messaging predicts reductions in smoking above and beyond self-report. Health Psychology 30: 177-185.

Genco, S.J., Pohlmann, A.P. and Steidl, P., 2013. Neuromarketing for dummies. Wiley and Sons, New York, NY, USA, 408 pp.

Gowans, C., 2015. Moral relativism. In: Zalta, E.N. (ed.) The stanford encyclopedia of philosophy. Fall 2015 edition. Available at: http://tinyurl.com/kogr7vz.

Greenfield, A., 2006. Everyware: the dawning of ubiquitous computing. New Riders, San Francisco, CA, USA, 272 pp.

Hartwig, V., Giovannetti, G., Vanello, N., Lombardi, M., Landini, L. and Simi, S., 2009. Biological effects and safety in magnetic resonance imaging: a review. International Journal of Environmental Research and Public Health 6: 1778-1798.

Health Library, 2016. Electroencephalogram (EEG). John Hopkins University. Available at: http://tinyurl.com/p7af97j.

International Chamber of Commerce (ICC) / ESOMAR, 2008. ICC/ESCOMAR international code on market and social research. ICC/ESOMAR, Paris / Amsterdam, France / the Netherlands.

International Chamber of Commerce (ICC), 2014. Codes centre for advertising and marketing. ICC. Available at: http://www.codescentre.com.

Ireland, D., 2006. Introductory note to Onfray. New Politics 10: 50.

Jacob, S.N., Shear, P.K., Norris, M., Smith, M., Osterhage, J., Strakowski, S.M., Cerullo, M., Fleck, D.E., Lee, J.-H. and Eliassen, J.C., 2015. Impact of functional magnetic resonance imaging (fMRI) scanner noise on affective state and attentional performance. Journal of Clinical and Experimental Neuropsychology 37: 563-570.

Jowitt, C. and Oakley-Brown, L., 2011. A pirate for all seasons? Captain Kidd and pirates in popular culture: a review of 'Pirates: the Captain Kidd story', an exhibition at the Museum of London Docklands, 20 May-30 October 2011. Journal for Maritime Research 13: 180-183.

Kamara, S., 2014. Is the NSA metadata program legal? Outsourced bits: a research blog on cloud computing, cryptography, security, privacy,.... Available at: http://tinyurl.com/k4s6adu.

Knuuti, J., Saraste, A., Kallio, M. and Minn, H., 2013. Is cardiac magnetic resonance imaging causing DNA damage? European Heart Journal 34: 2337-2339.

Kotler, P. and Zaltman, G., 1971. Social marketing: an approach to planned social change. Journal of Marketing 35(3): 3-12.

Leydesdorff, L., 2012. The triple helix, quadruple helix, ..., and an N-tuple of helices: explanatory models for analyzing the knowledge-based economy? Journal of the Knowledge Economy 3: 25-35.

Marsh, H., 1996. Below-the-line: walkers resurrects copycat brands war. Marketing 11.

Medicines and Healthcare products Regulatory 9MHRA), 2016. Welcome to the reporting site for the yellow card scheme. Medicines and Healthcare products Regulatory, London, UK. Available at: https://yellowcard.mhra.gov.uk.

Michman, R.D. and Mazze, E.M., 1998. The food industry wars: marketing triumphs and blunders. Greenwood Publishing Group, Quorum, USA, 263 pp.

Motycka, E.D., 2011. Development of an instrument to measure faculty adherence to the norms of science. PhD-thesis, Indiana State University, Terre Haute, IN, USA.

Murphy, L., 2011. ARF re:Think 2011: the great neuromarketing debate. Available at: http://tinyurl.com/k97bort.

Murphy, E.R., Illes, J. and Reiner, P.B., 2008. Neuroethics of neuromarketing. Journal of Consumer Behaviour 7: 293-302.

Neuromarketing Science and Business Association (NMSBA), 2013. The NMSBA code of ethics for the application of neuroscience in business. Available at: http://www.nmsba.com/ethics.

Neuromarketing Science and Business Association (NMSBA), 2016. The history of the NMSBA. Available at: http://www.nmsba.com/History.

NHS Choices, 2015. Food labels. NHS Choices blog. Available at: http://tinyurl.com/89lzvwl.

Oullier, O., 2012. Clear up this fuzzy thinking on brain scans. Nature 483: 7.

Phillipson, G., 2013. Q&A: the right to privacy. Religion and ethics. Available at: http://www.bbc.co.uk/religion/0/22887499.

Piqueras-Fiszman, B. and Spence, C., 2015. Sensory expectations based on product-extrinsic food cues: an interdisciplinary review of the empirical evidence and theoretical accounts. Food Quality and Preference 40, Part A: 165-179.

Plassmann, H., Venkatraman, V., Huettel, S. and Yoon, C., 2015. Consumer neuroscience: applications, challenges, and possible solutions. Journal of Marketing Research 52: 427-435.

Privacy International, 2016. What is metadata? Privacy international. Available at: https://www.privacyinternational.org/node/53.

Prochaska, J.O., 2008. Decision making in the transtheoretical model of behavior change. Medical Decision Making 28: 845-849.

Ramsøy, T.Z., 2013. Can you use the emotiv scales for anything? Brainethics (now Neurons Inc. Com). Available at: http://tinyurl.com/n7fbe9w.

Resnik, D.B., 2015. What is ethics in research and why is it important? U.S. Department of Health and Human Services, National Institute of Environmental Health Sciences. Available at: http://tinyurl.com/co2tu2n.

Retzios, A.D., 2009. Why do so many Phase 3 clinical trials fail. Issues in Clinical Research: Bay Clinical R&D Services.

Rey, H.G., Fried, I. and Quiroga, R.Q., 2014. Timing of single-neuron and local field potential responses in the human medial temporal lobe. Current Biology 24: 299-304.

Saba Jr., J.D., 2001. Internet property rights: E-trespass. St. Mary's Law Journal 33: 367.

Samuel, B., 2005. Not proven: introducing a third verdict. University of Chicago Law Review 72: 1299-1329.

Schnider, A., Von Däniken, C. and Gutbrod, K., 1996. The mechanisms of spontaneous and provoked confabulations. Brain 119: 1365-1375.

Shadlen, M.N. and Kiani, R., 2013. Decision making as a window on cognition. Neuron 80: 791-806.

Shapiro, D.L., 1988. Courts, legislatures, and paternalism. Virginia Law Review 74: 519-575.

Sidgwick, H., 1901. The method of ethics, 6th edition. Macmillan, London, UK, 568 pp.

Singh, S.P., 2005. Process of customer education and market creation. LBS Journal of Management and Research 3: 56-65.

Spool, A., 2015. Know your meme: the Mandela effect. Know Your Meme, Cheezburger Inc., New York, NY, USA.

Sunstein, C.R. and Thaler, R.H., 2012. Nudge: improving decisions about health, wealth and happiness. Penguin Books Limited, London, UK, 320 pp.

Tenetz, A., 2011. Artistic field work at the crossroads of DIY-technologies and tactical media art. In: Beloff, L., Berger, E. and Haapoja, T., (eds.) From landscape to laboratory, 1st edition. Finnish Society of Bioart, Helsinki, Finland, pp. 152-159.

Velasco, C., Wan, X., Salgado-Montejo, A., Woods, A., Oñate, G.A., Mu, B. and Spence, C., 2014. The context of colour-flavour associations in crisps packaging: a cross-cultural study comparing Chinese, Colombian, and British consumers. Food Quality and Preference 38: 49-57.

Vidal, J., 1997. McLibel: burger culture on trial. New Press, London, UK, 354 pp.

Voin, M., 2015. Questions and answers – Data protection reform. Fact Sheet, European Commission, Brussels, Belgium.

Voorhees Jr., T., Spiegel, D.L. and Cooper, D., 2011. Neuromarketing: legal and policy issues a Covington white paper. Covington and Burling LLP, Washington, DC, USA.

Wikipedia, 2016. Misfeasance. Wikipedia online, Wikimedia Foundation Inc., USA.

Wilson, R.M., Gaines, J. and Hill, R.P., 2008. Neuromarketing and consumer free will. Journal of Consumer Affairs 42: 389-410.

Zerzan, J. and Carnes, A., 1991. Questioning technology: tool, toy or tyrant? New Society Publishers, Gabriola Island, BC, USA, 222 pp.

Zerzan, J., 2005. Against civilization: readings and reflections. Feral House, Indiana University, Bloomington, IN, USA, 275 pp.

Zurawicki, L., 2010. Neuromarketing: exploring the brain of the consumer. Springer, Berlin, Germany, 273 pp.

Appendix: The NMSBA Code of Ethics

NMSBA Code of Ethics

The NMSBA Code of Ethics for the Application of Neuroscience in Business.

Adoption of this code is a condition of membership to the NMSBA. The code may be revised from time to time to ensure that it adequately reflects the highest ethical standards for the neuromarketing research industry. The NMSBA code accepts the principles enshrined in the ICC/ESOMAR code.

Definitions

1. **Neuromarketing Research**, is the systematic collection and interpretation of neurological and neurophysiological insights about individuals using different protocols allowing researchers to explore non-verbal and physiological responses to various stimuli for the purposes of market research.
2. **Neuromarketing Researcher** is defined as any individual or an organization carrying out, or acting as a Neuromarketing consultant on, a Neuromarketing research project, including those working in organizations buying services from a neuromarketing research company.
3. **Neuromarketing Client** is defined as any individual or organization that inquires, buys or sponsors or a Neuromarketing research project.
4. **Neuromarketing Research Participan**t is defined as any individual or an organization from which insights are collected using neuroscientific methods for the purposes of market research.
5. **Neuromarketing Study** is defined as a session with a participant during which Neuromarketing insights are collected.
6. **Neuromarketing Insights** are informed deductions supported by analyzing the amount of brain activity produced by marketing stimuli (advertisements, websites, packaging, etc.).
7. **Functional brain imaging** is defined as any technique that permits the in vivo visualization of the distribution of brain activity.

Articles
ARTICLE 1: CORE PRINCIPLES
a. Neuromarketing researchers shall comply with the highest research standards enforced in their respective countries and use accepted scientific principles.
b. Neuromarketing Researchers shall not act in any way that could negatively impact the reputation and the integrity of the Neuromarketing research profession.

c. Neuromarketing findings shall be delivered to clients without exaggerating or misrepresenting the neuromarketing insights beyond what is scientifically accepted.

ARTICLE 2: INTEGRITY

a. Neuromarketing researchers shall take all reasonable precautions to ensure that participants are in no way harmed or stressed as a result of their involvement in a Neuromarketing research project.
b. Neuromarketing researchers shall not deceive participants or exploit their lack of knowledge of neuroscience.
c. No sales offer shall be made to a participant as a direct result of his/her involvement in a project.
d. Neuromarketing researchers shall be honest about their skills and experience.

ARTICLE 3: CREDIBILITY

a. Concerns or critics about publicly known neuromarketing projects shall be first presented to the attention of the NMSBA before they are shared widely.
b. Neuromarketing researchers involved in functional brain imaging shall disclose a protocol for dealing with incidental findings.

ARTICLE 4: TRANSPARENCY

a. Participation in a Neuromarketing research project shall always be entirely voluntary.
b. Neuromarketing researchers shall maintain a public website describing their services and the credentials of their core team members as well as post a physical address where officers of the company can be contacted.
c. Neuromarketing researchers shall allow their clients to audit the process by which neuromarketing insights are collected and processed.
d. Neuromarketing researchers shall ensure that Neuromarketing research projects are created, delivered and documented with transparency and reported with as many details as the clients would require to understand the scope and relevance of the project.

ARTICLE 5: CONSENT

a. Neuromarketing researchers shall explain the tools they use to participants in layman terms.
b. Before providing consent, participants in Neuromarketing research shall explicitly express their understanding of the protocols as well as the general objectives of the study.
c. Participants shall be fully informed about the project before any Neuromarketing technique can be used to collect their neuromarketing insights.
d. Once a Neuromarketing study has commenced, participants shall be free to withdraw.

ARTICLE 6: PRIVACY

a. Neuromarketing researchers shall ensure that participants are made aware of the purpose of collecting insights.
b. Neuromarketing researchers shall have a privacy policy which is readily accessible to participants from whom they collect insights.
c. The identity of participants will not be revealed to the client without explicit consent.
d. Personal information collected shall be collected for specified Neuromarketing research purposes and not used for any other purpose.
e. Personal information may not be kept longer than is required for the purpose of the neuromarketing project.
f. Neuromarketing researchers shall ensure that adequate security measures are used to protect access to the insights collected during any project.
g. The Neuromarketing research data itself, including brain scans and brain data shall remain the property of the research company and will not be shared.

ARTICLE 7: PARTICIPANT RIGHTS

a. Participants to any neuromarketing research project shall confirm that they are not obligated to participate in the project.
b. Participants to any neuromarketing research project shall be able to withdraw from the research at any time.
c. Participants to any neuromarketing research project shall be guaranteed that their personal data is not made available to others.
d. Participants to any neuromarketing research project shall be guaranteed that the insights will be deleted or modified upon request.
e. Particular care shall be taken to maintain the data protection rights of participants when personal data is transferred from the country in which they are collected to another country. When data processing is conducted in another country, the data protection principles of this Code must be respected.

ARTICLE 8: CHILDREN AND YOUNG PEOPLE

Neuromarketing studies involving participants less than 18 years of age shall only take place with the informed consent of the participant's parents.

ARTICLE 9: SUBCONTRACTING

Neuromarketing Researchers shall disclose prior to work commencing, when any part of the project is to be subcontracted outside the neuromarketing researchers' own organization (including the use of any outside consultants).

ARTICLE 10: PUBLICATION

When results of a project are publicly shared, neuromarketing researchers shall clearly articulate which part of the report represents interpretation of the data vs which part of the data represent the key findings. Neuromarketing researchers shall not associate their names to a Neuromarketing research project unless they have actively participated in the project and are able to defend the findings

ARTICLE 11: COMMITMENT

Neuromarketing researchers shall commit that they will apply this code and ensure their own clients and other parties will comply with its requirements. Failure to do so will result in the termination of their membership.

ARTICLE 12: IMPLEMENTATION

a. Neuromarketing researchers and their clients shall acknowledge that they know the code and also respect other self-regulatory guidelines that are relevant to a particular region or project; The Code is applicable for all involved in a Neuromarketing project.
b. The NMSBA Members shall show their acceptance of the code, by publishing the code on their website or by publishing a link to www.nmsba.com/ethics (NMSBA, 2013).

4. Methods used in neuromarketing

J. Berčík* and J. Rybanská

Slovak University of Agriculture in Nitra, Faculty of Economics and Management, Department of Marketing and Trade, Tr. A. Hlinku 2, 949 76 Nitra, Slovak Republic; jakubstudio@gmail.com

Abstract

The current turbulent environment is associated with the re-evaluation of traditional methods and processes as well as the application of new information sources needed for the right decision-making of managers on all management levels, not only in manufacturing companies, but also services companies, not excluding business companies. In this chapter, we focus on the human nervous system in order to understand the human body producing signals subject to neuromarketing measurements better. Neuromarketing involves advanced measures, many of which have been applied and modified for decades in medicine and academic research. We also focus in detail on the signals obtained from the body (biometrics) and the brain (neuroimaging). Within each group we describe the most commonly used technologies and the principle of capturing signals and explain how these measurements can help better understanding of consumer behaviour, decision-making, and marketing management.

Keywords: innovative research solutions, neuroimaging methods, biometric methods

Learning objectives

After studying this chapter you should be able to:
- Understand the difference between measuring brain and biometric signals
- Decide on appropriate methods measuring brain and biometric signals according to research objective

4.1 Introduction to neuromarketing methods

Cognitive neuroscience as an academic discipline is increasingly growing and its research methods are continuously developing, providing unprecedented access to the structure and function of the brain. Their combination with theories from psychology, economics, and other disciplines enables creating new models of functions like memory, attention, emotion, and decision-making (Ruff and Huettel, 2014). All these methods have become both more refined and more accessible to the research community.

Neuromarketing technologies have created the profiling discipline of marketing research, which for some people questions the traditional boundaries of privacy and even the very concept of 'free will' (Feinberg et al., 2012). Adoption of new technologies from the field of neuroscience and consumer behaviour into the conventional market research, however, represents a significant investment today, in terms of fully understanding and meeting the objectives of the research topic.

Neuromarketing research is based on a model that explains how people use their brain for understanding, explaining, and influencing the outside world. This model divides the brain operations into four basic activities (Genco et al., 2013):
- forming impressions;
- determining the meaning and value;
- reflecting and analysing; and
- speaking and acting.

> The activity of the nervous system is provided by the central nervous system (CNS) and the peripheral nervous system (PNS). The central nervous system consists of the brain and spinal cord, and carries out only two activities from the model (determining the meaning and value, reflecting and analysing) and it is also responsible for decision-making. The other two activities from the model (forming impressions, speaking and acting) are included in the peripheral nervous system, which consists of sensory input systems (nerves that communicate the sensory inputs of the brain) and motor systems (receive commands from the brain and communicate them to the muscles and glands).

Two fundamental differences in the nervous system are important for understanding the origin and the methods of particular neuromarketing measurements:

The first difference between the CNS and PNS (or simply between the brain and body) is that brain measurements in neuromarketing focus on capturing the activity controlled by the CNS within the brain, whereas the body measurements aim to capture physical reactions (muscle movement) controlled by the brain through the PNS.

The second significant difference in terms of neuromarketing measurements is that the motor commands made by the PNS may be communicated through the somatic nervous system (SNS) or the autonomic nervous system (ANS). This difference is also significant due to the fact that the signals from ANS are relatively slow and largely automatic, while they represent responses such as breathing, heart rate, sweating, and dilated pupils. The signals coming from the CIS are much faster, and to the extent possible at least partially controlled. These are responses such as facial expressions, eye movements, blinking, and behavioural reactions (Genco *et al.*, 2013).

Accordingly, it is possible to divide the research tools and techniques of neuromarketing into two main categories (Table 4.1): biometric measurement (measuring the reactions of the body) and brain measurement (measuring the response of the brain) under the influence of marketing stimuli. Each approach captures a different type of signal and each brings a number of various advantages and disadvantages depending on the used measurement technique.

Table 4.1. Neuromarketing measures from the body and the brain (based on Genco *et al.*, 2013, pp. 252).

Body measures		Brain measures	
somatic nervous system measures	Autonomic nervous system measures	Blood flow measures	Electrical measures
facial expressions	electrodermal activity	blood oxygenation (functional magnetic resonance imaging)	electrical fields (electroencephalography)
facial muscle movements	heart rate	Positron emissions tomography	Magnetic encephalography
eye movements and fixations	blood pressure		
eye blinks and the startle reflex	respiration		
behavioural response times	pupil dilation		

Neuromarketing research can be classified from different perspectives:

- according to the methods of obtaining information:
  - primary;
  - secondary;
- according to the approach to reactions:
  - biometric;
  - brain;
  - combination;
- according to the place of conducting the research:
  - simulated conditions (laboratory);
  - real conditions (stores, outdoor, services companies);
  - online (online panel studies, social media);
- according to the type of imaging technology:
  - stationary devices:
    - invasive technologies;
    - non-invasive technologies;
  - mobile devices:
    - invasive technologies;
    - non-invasive technologies;
- according to the institution conducting the research:
  - academic;
  - commercial;
- according to the orientation to stimuli:
  - sensory neuroresearch;
  - marketing (4P / 4C) neuroresearch;
- according to the object of the research:
  - research of marketing mix;
  - research of consumer behaviour.

4.2 Methods of measuring brain signals

Neurological (neurometric) indicators (based on signals from the brain) are more complex, but also more accurate and detailed than biometric parameters. In the case of these measurements, it may happen that the efforts and costs of the use of the techniques needed to conduct neuroresearch are often higher than the contribution of relevant information. Nevertheless, it should be emphasized that it is primarily a question of correctly setting the research objectives and selecting technologies.

When determining which research method to use, three factors are of primary importance: temporal resolution (frequency in time for measurements), spatial resolution (the ability to distinguish differently functioning brain parts), and invasiveness (whether the measurement can be made without damage to or disruption of the brain or other body tissue) (Ruff and Huettel, 2014).

Technologies which measure brain activity are often referred to as neuroimaging technologies, because they include images or pictures presenting brain activity. Different techniques offer complementary information, e.g. in the form of detailed spatial maps of function or showing very rapid changes in activity when those functions are engaged.

According to another division these measurements can be divided into two main categories: the measurement of blood flow and electrical measurement.

4.2.1 The measurement of blood flow

The measurement of blood flow reflects the brain activity based on localizing the increased blood flow which is essential for the supply of energy (oxygen and glucose) for activated neurons.

Functional magnetic resonance imaging

Functional magnetic resonance imaging (fMRI) is a derived variant of magnetic resonance imaging (MRI). Its concept is based on a conventional MRI scanner, but it also records two other phenomena – blood perfusion (flow) and oxygen supply (Zurawicki, 2010). This method is a popular tool of academic researchers and currently it can be considered the most widespread in the research of cognitive functions, emotions, and personal qualities. The fMRI device measures the blood flow (perfusion) and oxygen supply in different parts of the human brain through a three-dimensional image of the brain, the so-called BOLD effect (blood oxygenation level dependent) (Fandelová and Kačániová, 2012).

Detection of the brain activity by this method is based on the fact that the oxygenated blood contains hydrogen protons (iron), which are oxygen carrying components of the hemoglobin, and which can be recognized through a massive magnet surrounding the head of the subject being measured. Due to changes in the blood oxygenation and local flow it is possible to indirectly detect those parts of the cortex which are involved in carrying out cognitive, motor, or other tasks performed by the measured subject (Turner and Sahakian, 2006). This method is based on the assumption that the active part of the brain uses more oxygen from the blood to function correctly (Gregorová, 2009). When dealing with specific incentives, such as an advertisement, a certain area acquires more oxygenated blood than during the rest period. Such a change causes distortion of the magnetic field.

Although each year over 2000 new fMRI studies of diverse topics are investigated – covering everything from memory and perception to altruism and moral decision-making – there is no typical fMRI study. Most involve many repeated trials to improve the signal-to-noise ratio associated with the effects of interest. The physical environment of the scanner (possibly loud and confining) limits what participants can perceive and do, however, within those limitations almost any experimental design can be introduced for fMRI research (Hunt *et al.*, 2012).

Morin (2011) sums up the advantages and disadvantages of this method. The advantages are as follows:
▸ the ability to gather large amount of information;
▸ the ability to create a picture of the deep brain structures;
▸ the ability to recognize genuine emotional reactions (limbic system);
▸ no aggressive effects (no radiation or other side effects).

Disadvantages of this method include:
▸ financially, spatially, and time demanding;
▸ the need for professional service;
▸ providing results with a few seconds delay;
▸ limited sample of the surveyed subjects.

Positron emission tomography

Positron emission tomography (PET) is a brain imaging procedure through recording radiation from positron emissions, which are small atomic particles from a radioactive substance that is served to the respondent (Zurawicki, 2010). Positrons (anti-electrons) are antiparticles of electrons, which have a positive electric charge and the same weight as electrons. After injecting or inhaling a small amount of these modified molecules we observe their spatial distribution using PET scanner. This device is sensitive to the radiation of positrons, which come into contact with ubiquitous electrons in the human body and produce small gamma radiation when clashing. This enables a relatively quick and easy mapping of human brain activity. The PET scanner then creates tomograms based on this information (Kenning and Plassmann, 2005). Using PET scanner requires detailed logistical planning and brings also some technical problems related to the application of radioactive material and its short life. Similarly as fMRI, the PET examination method is very costly, which greatly limits the size of the survey sample and subsequent generalization of results.

PET research within cognitive neuroscience is mainly conducted with human participants, who in the laboratory first complete safety and consent forms, and then enter the PET scanner. The researchers either inject the isotope before scanning (e.g. in the case of radioactive glucose, an hour before) or during scanning (e.g. with some chemicals that bind to neurotransmitter receptors). PET can be used to study a variety of neurobiological processes with one major difference compared with other techniques: PET aggregates emission events over long time windows (several minutes), therefore experiments are organized into long block of time (Ruff and Huettel, 2014).

Functional Transcranial Doppler

Functional transcranial Doppler (fTCD)is a neurosonological examination method. It is an ultrasound examination that allows non-invasive imaging of blood flow through the arteries, cerebral veins, and sinuses through the intact skull in real time. It can identify parts of the brain that are involved in certain economic behaviour. Duplex sonography can also be used in an environment outside the laboratory, as this test does not load the studied subject, it is easy and fast. Other advantages are portability and relatively low price (Světlík, 2012).

4.2.2 Electrical measurement

Electrical measurement directly captures the electrical and magnetic activity consisting of activated neurons.

Electroencephalography

Electroencephalography (EEG) is a technology which is using small, but highly sensitive microsensors, used for measuring the current in the top layer of the cerebral cortex, therefore it does not provide information about the subcortical brain activity (Palokangas, 2010).

Measurement of cortical electrical brain activity (activity of neurons in the upper part of the cerebral cortex) is still the most applied neuromarketing method in terms of cost and demand of conducting the research. This method aims to examine the impact of stimuli on the changes in the electrical brain activity of the surveyed subjects. Electrodes applied to the scalp are recording 2,000 times a second a very low electric current from the brain fields, generated by the rapid movement of neurons under the impact of nerve impulses (Berčík *et al.*, 2014). The frequent use of this technology in research benefits from the massive support of scientific literature. The biggest limitation of EEG is that changes in the electrical activity deep in the brain cannot be reliably measured. There are stationary or mobile devices, the usability of which partly differs depending on the number of channels. Each part of the brain is responsible for a particular function, and therefore the use of more affordable devices that do not have a sufficient number of sensors causes lack of the basic element of connectivity and in fact insufficient results in terms of accepted neurological standards (Pradeep, 2010).

When doing the experiment, firstly the participant completes some documents and then practises the experimental task while the electrodes are placed (there is the possibility to use caps with pre-positioned electrodes to speed up the process). The experimental task is done repeatedly, often within 30 to 120 minutes periods. EEG provides good temporal resolution. Experimental trials can be run very rapidly, one after the other. After data collection about brain activity measured in precise time windows, algorithm processing is applied to minimize data quality issues and trial-by-trial responses from each electrode analysed. In order to improve statistical power, most EEG studies combine data from 10-40 respondents (Ruff and Huettel, 2014).

The advantages of this method are (Nagyová *et al.*, 2014):
▸ not financially, spatially, and time demanding;
▸ massive support from scientific literature;
▸ providing results in real time;
▸ the availability of mobile versions.

Disadvantages of this method include:
▸ the possibility of measuring the electrical activity deep in the brain (subcortical brain activity) is absent;
▸ the need for specialized staff when interpreting the results;
▸ difference in the electrical conductivity of the surveyed subjects;
▸ irrationality of the assumptions that brain impulses arise only based on certain stimuli.

Steady-state topography (SST) is a modern version of EEG, which monitors the fast brain waves in real time. An advantage of the SST in comparison to the EEG is that this method is less sensitive to the effects of the body and eye movement during the measurement (Broekhoff, 2014). It processes the signals from the sensors in the 'cap' on the head. The signal is recorded 13 times a second and processed by a computer.

Magnetic encephalography

Magnetic encephalography (MEG) has some advantages compared to EEG (as opposed to the electric current in the magnetic field, it is not affected by the tissues) and is used mainly in academic studies, as its practical application in commercial neuromarketing is not considered successful. The reason for this is the significant financial and operational complexity of this device (including a demanding cooling) (Světlík, 2012). The device allows to measure electric currents in the brain by very small changes of the magnetic field and is a direct measure of the brain activity compared to other methods (such as fMRI and PET), which reflect the secondary brain activity, reflecting its metabolism (e.g. oxygen demand). Superconducting sensors detect the magnetic fields around the head caused by neuronal activity (Vysekalová *et al.,* 2011). Magnetic encephalography is the only method that can estimate the impact of external stimuli on the brain activity. It is used to monitor the brain activity of people watching television commercials or receiving various other visual stimuli.

In a MEG experiment, the participant sits upright in the MEG system. Compared to the MRI, the conditions are relatively open and natural. The participant watches the experimental stimuli on a screen in front of him (a projector is placed outside the room to minimalize magnetic interference) and responds using a button box or keyboard positioned in his lap. Compared to the other techniques, MEG has been less commonly used in neuromarketing research (Ruff and Huettel, 2014).

Fandelová and Kačániová (2012) present the advantages and disadvantages of this method. The advantages include:
- fast and accurate recording of changes due to stimuli;
- the ability to gather large amount of information;
- excellent spatial resolution with millimetre accuracy.

Disadvantages of this method can be described as follows:
- financially, spatially, and operationally demanding;
- the need for professional service;
- signals of interest are very small compared to other methods.

Although MRI is good on detail, it is too slow to chart fast-moving events. Both EEG and MEG are fast but are not as good at identifying location. In order to get scans that show both fast processes and location, it is necessary to use two or more methods for a combined image (Carter *et al.,* 2014).

4.3 Methods of measuring biometric signals

Biometrics is a universal concept that involves measurements of physiological responses of the body – not directly the brain – to the external stimuli that are perceived through the senses. The most widely used biometric measures for neuromarketing include cardiac and respiratory activity, eye movement, blinking, galvanic skin response (GSR), facial expressions, and body movements. Some biometric measurements are limited for the purposes of market research, because they are delayed indicators (indirect measurements) of primary brain activity, since the brain may issue a command for the body well in advance before there is a physiological effect. The ideal case is to know when the brain issues an order, not its actual implementation (Pradeep, 2010).

Biometric measurements can be divided into measurements of somatic functions and measurements of autonomic functions.

4.3.1 Measurements of somatic functions

Measurements of somatic functions can, at least, be partially influenced.

Facial expressions

A whole range of emotional states is recognizable on the human face. Changes in facial expressions can be classified on two levels: observable changes of expressions – microemotions (e.g. a smile or scowl) and unobservable changes of mimic muscles (e.g. muscle contraction associated with positive and negative emotional response). Observing facial expressions appears to be an important indicator of positive or negative emotional reactions – valence. To detect observable changes in facial expressions a special software (Facereader) is used (Figure 4.1), which can very quickly detect emotions from the recorded face of the surveyed subject. Unobservable changes in the electrical activity of mimic muscles can be monitored through electromyography, which by sensors registers the action potential (excitement) caused by deliberate activation of a muscle or irritation of a peripheral nerve.

Eye tracking

Measuring eye movements and dilated pupils when viewing the subject, object, or scene has multiple uses in neuromarketing, both as a separate tool, but also as an important complement to other indicators. The speed and the sight direction change provide valuable indicators of attention, interest, and attraction. The device for measuring eye movement is called Eye tracker, and there are mobile and fixed versions of the device based on the nature of the conducted research. Eye tracking offers market researchers the possibility to collect specific data that can be statistically analysed and graphically rendered, thus increasing the quality of their research (http://tinyurl.com/luk8qnf).

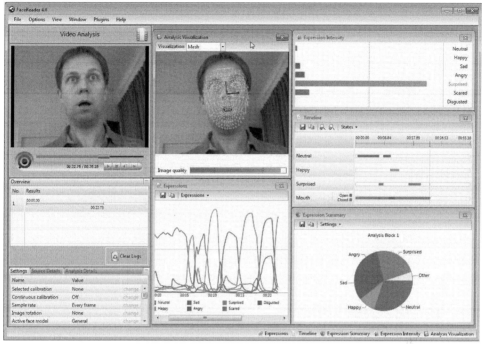

Figure 4.1. Software for reading observable facial expressions from the company Noldus (MSH, 2016).

Response time

One way of how the subconscious brain processes are revealed in the behaviour is measuring the response speed of the nervous system to verbal associations or visual cues. The rate of response time provides a simple and available way of testing the strength of association between different concepts. Currently neuromarketers already successfully use this method of measurement in testing the brand, product, and packaging.

4.3.2 Measurements of autonomic functions

Measurements of autonomic functions cannot be influenced and happen automatically.

Electrodermal activity

Electrodermal activity (EDA) concerns measuring changes in skin resistance due to sweating. The first findings about the electrical properties of the skin appeared in the 19th century and are still used today. Electrical phenomena of the skin (skin conductance changes) associated with the activity of the sweat glands are called psychogalvanic reflexes (PGRs). To understand them it is necessary to know the basics of anatomy and skin physiology, as well as technical requirements of measuring them. PGR is a change of the electrical properties of the body (especially the skin) caused by certain stimulus that triggers an emotional response (unexpected noise, painful shocks, affectogenic words, anxiety, stress, etc.). The response appears as an increase in the electrical skin conductivity (decrease in resistance) across the palms or soles. The response is not immediate, it occurs approximately 2 seconds after the stimulation, reaching a maximum 2-10 seconds later and likewise it also quickly subsides. The sympathetic part of the autonomic nervous system is responsible for the reflex (Nakonečný, 2000, pp. 153). EDA is a good indicator of the reticular activation and reflects energy dimensions of behaviour and in particular of emotional experience. Electrodermal response amplitude linearly increases with rising excitement, regardless the valence of emotions (Bradley and Lang, 2000). PGRs are an important and often followed indicator of the presence of emotions, because they are one of the most sensitive indicators of minimum emotional arousal or activation. The PGR is essentially involuntary and often used as one of the indicators on the lie detector, along with blood pressure, pulse, and respiration. This category includes devices that measure GSR (GSR device) or EDA of the skin (EDA device). These devices are technically undemanding, therefore they can be used in laboratory as well as in real research conditions. Sweating can be monitored not only as PGRs, but also directly on the surface of the body using a variety of chemical methods and mechanical procedures. Usually it is detected using filter papers, as the perspiration changes their colour (Nakonečný, 2000, pp. 155; Trávničková, 2012, pp. 13).

For more than 70 years, marketers are trying to reliably evaluate the effectiveness of different marketing communication tools. One of the oldest and most widely used tools to measure emotional reactions of consumers is a GSR device that finds its applicability in the academic, medical, and commercial sphere. It is most commonly used to assess a television or radio advertising. It provides evidence that it is possible to capture excitement (emotional reactions) of consumers when they are watching a marketing message. The oldest GSR researches focused on the phasic component of ongoing tonic response. The findings show that the absence of a stimulus causes the gradual decrease of tonic response. Monitoring tonic and phasic patterns of each subject when watching 40 advertisements, mainly of food products, helped reveal a lot of information about the human personality and temperament. A research with the GSR device revealed that introverts, mostly those with anxious tendencies, are the hardest convincible market segment. Using the GSR device it was also found that advertisements with more cuts are less attractive to consumers and more difficult to recall (Shimmel, 2002).

Breathing

Monitoring changes in breathing, respiratory rate, depth of inhalation, and exhalation. Changes occur due to different factors causing emotions of varying intensity and valence. The rhythm of breathing changes due to affects, when it especially accelerates and becomes irregular. Changes in breathing are measured with pneumograph or linked to a measurement of autonomic functions (Nakonečný, 2000, pp. 154). For measuring the respiratory activity in neuromarketing, respirometer is used, which is fastened around the waist of the surveyed subject and reflects the quality of his breathing. Fast and deep breathing is associated with enthusiasm, while shallow breathing may indicate concentration, tense expectation, or panic and fear. Since these are relatively affordable and available technologies, they can be used not only in simulated, but also in real research conditions.

Heart rate and blood pressure

Heart rate and blood pressure are other indicators of the onset of an emotion. Most often changes in the heartbeat rhythm and heart rate (pulse) are monitored (Figure 4.2). Heart rate is the number of beats per minute. For a healthy heart at standstill 60 to 100 beats per

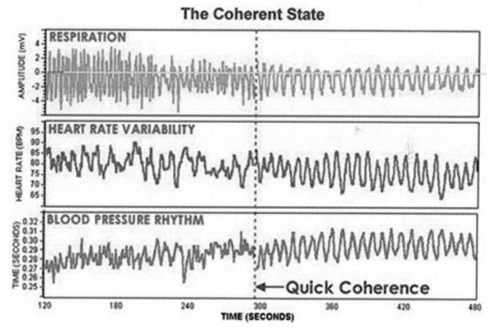

Figure 4.2. The analysis of breathing, heartbeat variability and blood pressure (HeartMath, 2011).

minute is considered the optimum number (Nakonečný, 2000, pp. 154). Heartbeat increases in a state of excitement and slows down with the upcoming calmness. It was also found that the heart rate significantly slows down at the moment when the attention of the respondent is increasing. To measure the pulse, most commonly pulsemeter and oximeter are used, which measure the amount of oxygen in the blood using infrared light. Electrocardiograph is used for monitoring cardiac activity and its changes. Today, an analysis of heart rate variability is also used in neuromarketing. Emotions also affect the pattern of the heart rhythm. The analysis of heart rate variability or heart rhythms is an established and decisive non-invasive indicator of how the connection between the brain and heart functions. It also reflects the dynamics of the autonomic nervous system, which is particularly sensitive to changes in emotional states. Heart rate variability biofeedback monitors heart rate variability (Figure 4.3). The base of the technology is measuring changes (increase and decrease) of the heart rate between two heartbeats (Balog, 2011). Blood pressure is along with cardiac activity and PGR the best indicator of the onset of activation (emotion). With the onset of affects the blood pressure (both systolic and diastolic) increases. Electrodermal and cardiovascular responses reliably predict the level of activation and valence of emotional stimuli (Bradley and Lang, 2000).

> When surveying the willingness of consumers to take risks when purchasing wines we found through monitoring cardiac cycle and heart rate variability that consumers prefer high-quality wine that is recommended by experts in 97% of cases.
>
> (Beranek *et al.*, 2013)

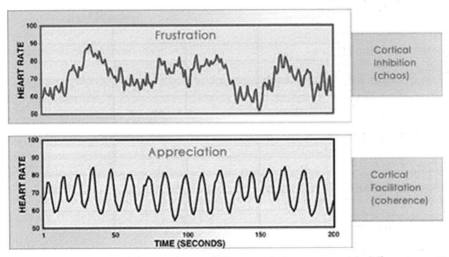

Figure 4.3. Heart rate variability analysis – differences in heart rate with different emotions (HeartMath, 2011).

Dilated pupils (pupillary reflex)

Eye pupil dilation and narrowing. Under strong excitement, fear, pain, but also when looking at an exciting sexual object, the pupil dilates as an effect of the sympathetic part of the autonomic nervous system. Pupil dilation or narrowing, however, also occurs when the eye accommodates to light, thus as an effect of non-emotional stimuli (Nakonečný, 2000, pp. 154). Pupillary responses are observable within a few milliseconds after the presentation or the influence of stimuli (Beatty, 1986). The pupillary reflex is measured with a special device called pupilometer.

4.4 Combining multiple research methods into a single unit

Based on the advantages and disadvantages of various methods used in neuromarketing research, a combination (Figure 4.4) of at least some of them may, depending on the nature of the research problem, produce excellent results, as opposed to the orientation on just one

Figure 4.4. Mobile eye tracker (Tobii) and mobile electroencephalography (Emotiv).

particular technology. The implementation of different measures at the same time saves the time of the research participants and a range of procedures (Zurawicki, 2010).

Example

LABoratory – a company from Poland dealing with market research – uses three types of devices when examining responses to television advertising. Electromyography records the voluntary and involuntary movements of facial muscles, reflecting the conscious and subconscious expression of emotions (positive vs negative emotions). EEG measurements confirm emotional valence and control whether multimedia presentation raises semantic attention to the words. Finally, the skin resistance sensor records the level of excitement.

The combination of different methods is also used in a technology developed by scientists from the Slovak University of Agriculture (SUA) in Nitra. The technology of a special shopping cart designed for field research will bring more information to the understanding of the decision-making process under the impact of external factors of the shopping environment (Figure 4.5), because it combines in addition to neuroimaging and biometric methods also a measurement of the factors of the environment and manipulation of the shopping cart.

Figure 4.5. Special shopping cart for neuromarketing field research.

New technologies are an important part of the new world of neuromarketing, but not the most important one. Neuromarketing research providers damage their clients in cases when they point to technological issues more than to the problems companies have in the field of marketing and sales communications.

Example

fMRI studies providers like to say that the use of EEG is like trying to watch a football match while standing outside the stadium. Conversely, EEG providers like to respond that the use of fMRI is like taking photos of a football match after the game ended. In a sense both are correct arguments, but exaggerate the limits of technologies, because both technologies provide ground-breaking discoveries and knowledge of the brain that are supported by thousands of active researches worldwide.

The value of neuromarketing research is primarily a function of fulfilling three aspects:
- defining the right research question;
- identifying (selecting) correct measurements of consumer responses;
- designing the right test for the specific research question.

EEG and fMRI are among the most reliable indicators of consumer responses, because they can immediately monitor changes in the brain and the activity of various brain centres. Very often a research using these devices focuses on the influence of sensory stimuli on consumer reactions, especially the impact of visual and auditory stimuli. Taste stimuli are often associated with other sensory stimuli, especially olfactory and visual. Studies using these devices have found out, for example, that consumers indicate high-calorie and fatty foods as the most attractive, as these affect the human brain in a way that is very similar to the effect of cocaine or heroin. These foods activate dopamine release exactly the same way as the mentioned drugs, the dependence on calorie food can be therefore compared with drug addiction. It was also found that the effects of addiction to unhealthy diet last about seven times longer than the effects of cocaine or heroin addiction. Other highly addictive substances include salt, monosodium glutamate, sugar, certain sweeteners, colouring agents, caffeine, and menthol. Consumers evaluate foods containing any of these substances more positively (Lindstrom, 2011; Mirmiran *et al.*, 2010).

References

Balog, A., 2011. Psychoterapia, biofeedback. Available at: http://tinyurl.com/l48beyk.

Beatty, J., 1986. The pupillary system. In: Coles, M.G.H., Donchin, E. and Porges, S.W. (eds.) Psychophysiology: systems, processes, and applications. Guilford Press, New York, NY, USA, pp. 43-50.

Beranek, C., Halfmann, K., Kurczek, J. and Hedgcock, W., 2013. Use of heart rate and heart rate variability in decision making research. Available at: http://tinyurl.com/ky4770g.

Berčík, J., Paluchová, J., Kleinová, K., Horská, E. and Nagyová, Ľ., 2014. Stimulus, space and hidden customer's reactions: applying possibilities of neuromarketing. In: Zentková, I. (ed.) Improving performance of agriculture and the economy: challenges for management and policy: international scientific days 2014. 13th International Conference, May 21-23, 2014, High Tatras, Slovak Republic, 138 pp.

Bradley, M.M. and Lang, P.J., 2000. Measuring emotion: behavior, feeling and physiology. In: Lane, R.D., Nadel, L. and Geoffrey, A. (eds.) Cognitive neuroscience of emotion. Oxford University Press, Oxford, UK, pp. 242-276.

Broekhoff, M., 2014. Conceptual closure can kill television ads. Neuromarketing Theory and Practice 9: 10-11.

Carter, R., Aldridge, S., Page, M. and Parker, S., 2014. The human brain book. DK Publishing, New York, NY, USA, 264 pp.

Fandelová, E. and Kačániová, M., 2012. Analýza aktuálnych trendov marketingovej komunikácie – neuromarketing, 25 pp. Available at: http://tinyurl.com/k3p6fkm.

Feinberg, F.M., Kinnear, T.C. and Taylor, J.R., 2012. Modern marketing research: concepts, methods, and cases. South-Western, Cengage Learning, Mason, OH, USA, 720 pp.

Genco, S.J., Pohlmann, A.P. and Steidl, P., 2013. Neuromarketing for dummies. John Wiley and Sons, Mississauga, Canada, 408 pp.

Gregorová, D., 2009. Výsledky sú super, len tá štatistika bola nesprávna. Available at: http://www.osel.cz/tisk.php?clanek=4390.

HeartMath, 2011. What is heart rate variability and coherence? Available at: http://www.torquerelease.com.au/emWave.htm.

Hunt, L.T., Kolling, N., Soltani, A., Woolrich, M.W., Rushworth, M.F. and Behrens, T.E., 2012. Mechanisms underlying cortical activity during value-guided choice. Nature Neuroscience 15(3): 470-476.

Kenning, P. and Plassmann, H., 2005. NeuroEconomics: an overview from an economic perspective. 2nd Conference on NeuroEconomics – ConNEcs 2004. Brain Research Bulletin 67(5): 343-354.

Lindstrom, M., 2011. Brandwashed: tricks companies use to manipulate our minds and persuade us to buy. Crown Business, Kogan Page Limited, London, UK, 304 pp.

Mirmiran, P., Fazeli, M.R., Asghari, G., Shafiee, A. and Azizi, F., 2010. Effect of pomegranate seed oil on hyperlipidaemic subjects: a double-blind placebo-controlled clinical trial. British Journal of Nutrition 104(3): 402-406.

Morin, Ch., 2011. Neuromarketing: the new science of consumer behavior. Society 48(2): 131-135.

MSH – Maison des Sciences de l'Homme, 2016. SCREEN: Service commun de ressources pour l'expérimentation et l'équipement numérique. Solution de reconnaissance des émotions faciales. FaceReader. Available at: http://tinyurl.com/mmjyazj.

Nagyová, Ľ., Horská, E., Kretter, A., Kubicová, Ľ., Košičiarová, I., Récky, R., Berčík, J. and Holienčinová, M., 2014. Marketing. Slovak University of Agriculture, Nitra, Slovak Republic, 460 pp.

Nakonečný, M., 2000. Lidské emoce. Academia, Prague, Czech Republic, 336 pp.

Palokangas, L., 2010. Measuring the willingness to purchase using methods of neuromarketing. Laurea University of Applied Sciences, Finland, 108 pp. Available at: http://tinyurl.com/l7n7786.

Pradeep, A.K., 2010. The buying brain: secrets for selling to the subconscious mind. John Wiley and Sons, Hoboken, NJ, USA, 272 pp.

Ruff, Ch.C. and Huettel, S.A., 2014. Experimental methods in cognitive neuroscience. In: Glimcher, P.W. and Fehr, E. (eds.) Neuroeconomics: decision making and the brain. Academic Press, London, UK, pp. 77-108.

Shimmel, J., 2002. Testing ads using skin conductance response measurements. Available at: http://tinyurl.com/m9354kg.

Světlík, J., 2012. O podstatě reklamy. Eurokódex, Bratislava, Slovak Republic, 312 pp.

Trávničková, H., 2012. Kožní odpor a psychogalvanický reflex. Vysoké učení technické v Brně, Brno, Czech Republic, 45 pp.

Turner, D.C. and Sahakian, B.J., 2006. Ethical questions in functional neuroimaging and cognitive enhancement. Poiesis and Praxis 4(2): 81-94.

Vysekalová, J. et al., 2011. Chování zákazníka: jak odkrýt tajemství 'černé skříňky'. Grada, Prague, Czech Republic, 356 pp.

Zurawicki, L., 2010. Neuromarketing: exploring the brain of the consumer. Springer-Verlag Berlin Heidelberg, Germany, 273 pp.

5. Application of neuromarketing in communication with the customer

B. Borusiak[1]*, B. Pierański[1], D. Brohm[2] and N. Domurath[2]

[1]Poznań University of Economics and Business, Department of Commerce and Marketing, Al. Niepodległości 10, 61-875 Poznan, Poland; [2]INTEGAR – Institut für Technologien im Gartenbau GmbH, Schlüterstraße 29, 01277 Dresden, Germany; barbara.borusiak@ue.poznan.pl

Abstract

The aim of this chapter is to classify and characterise the tools of communication with the customer, considering the possibilities of using neuromarketing methods to identify consumer needs and wants and satisfy them as good as possible. The impact of in-store communication tools on customer behaviour is difficult to ascertain by means of traditional methods, based on the opinions expressed by buyers. Better results can be obtained using methods based on observation, such as neuromarketing methods, which are principally used for examining the influence of visual merchandising techniques on customer behaviour. In case of online communication the tracking technologies are able to save and analyse every click, every visited page, every sold item, the dwell time on pages and even the gestures of the computer mouse. By creating user specific or target group specific profiles the companies are in the situation to influence the purchase decision in every phase of the buying process.

Keywords: in-store communication, retailer's marketing instruments, visual merchandising techniques, online purchase decisions

Learning objectives

After studying this chapter you should be able to:
- ▶ Discuss the application of neuromarketing in in-store communications techniques
- ▶ Discuss the application of neuromarketing in online communication techniques

5.1 Nature and objectives of in-store communication

In-store communication is primarily a component in the promotional activities of retailers. Retail promotion can be defined as any communication that informs, influences and prompts the target market about any aspect of the retail sponsor (Gilbert, 1999). In-store communication can also be used by manufacturers who use retail companies in the process of product distribution.

The characteristic features of in-store communication (regardless of the entity using this communication channel) are as follows:
► relatively long exposure time to the communication, in some cases equivalent to the time the customer spends in the store;
► limited possibilities for the customer to avoid the transmitted message (as is the case with channel zapping in relation to television advertising, or installing AdBlock software to block online advertising);
► accompanying character of the impact: the customer receives the message while doing shopping, their attention is usually not focused on the communicated information;
► low level of awareness as to the impact exerted by means of a range of instruments, especially non-verbal ones;
► indirect nature of the impact by many instruments, generating mainly image-related effects.

According to the hierarchical concept of business strategy, the objectives of the communication strategies directed at consumers are not autonomous but result from the objectives of the marketing strategy. Generally, these objectives can be both quantitative and qualitative, and this is reflected in the objectives of in-store communication.

The quantitative objectives in retailing include those that are measured by the level and structure of sales:
► the achieved rate and amount of profit margin;
► the amount of profit
► the profitability of sales;
► the number of customers;
► the number of transactions;
► average transaction value;
► the level of customer retention (percentage of customers making repeat purchases) which is a manifestation of behavioural loyalty;
► the frequency of customers' visits.

The major qualitative objectives relate to achieving the desired image (e.g. a cheap shop, a luxury shop, a shop suitable for everyday shopping, a shop which satisfies comprehensive needs, etc.) as well as generating an awareness of the store's brand and the own labels which a given store offers (Gilbert, 1999).

5.2 Classification of the forms of in-store communications

The forms of in-store communication can be classified according to several criteria as it is shown in Table 5.1.

As regards manufacturers, communication with the customers through a store is part of the so-called BTL (Below The Line) activities, i.e. those which are implemented without the aid of traditional media (press, radio, television). Manufacturers communicate with customers through retail stores in the following ways:

▸ product presentations and sampling;
▸ trade promotions, i.e. activities addressed to the sales staff of the intermediary in the distribution channel (training, motivating);
▸ consumer promotions, consisting of a short-term increase in the attractiveness of an offer, mainly through temporary price reductions (e.g. two products for the price of one);
▸ the way of presenting products in a store, including product placement, the type of display used, and the arrangement of products;

Table 5.1. Classification of in-store communication forms.

Criterion for classification	Forms of communication	Examples of tools
Agent of communication	Manufacturer's communication	Presentations, trade promotions, consumer promotions, product displays, POS materials
	Retailer's communication	Consumer promotions, store layout, in-store music, store design
Mechanism of impact	Direct communication	Advertisements, advertising posters and leaflets, digital signage, promotional displays
	Indirect communication	Colour scheme, prices and price tags, product assortment and displays
Medium of communication	Personal communication	Personal selling, in-store sampling with hosts/hostesses
	Impersonal communication	Type, colour and intensity of light, methods of displaying merchandise, type of store displays

► point-of-sale materials, which comprise a range of diverse audio, visual, audio-visual and printed advertising; including posters, leaflets, wobblers, shelf-talkers, shelf-liners, hangers, dummy packs, light boxes, stickers and window stickers, counter cards, and many others.

In-store retailer's communication comprises a much broader set of tools, which is a simple consequence of the ability to control all the elements constituting a store. In general, these instruments can be categorised on the basis of two criteria: the mechanism of impact and the medium of communication. In view of the subject matter of this book, this chapter focuses on impersonal instruments of indirect impact, among which a group of visual merchandising tools have been distinguished. These will be discussed later in this chapter.

5.3 Retailer's marketing instruments as forms of communication

5.3.1 Selection of assortment

Product assortment in retail is a deliberately selected set of goods offered for sale. This is one of the retail marketing instruments which determine the retail format, and, to a large extent, also the remaining instruments; namely the pricing policy, the location of a store, as well as the communication policy treated as a separate tool. The assortment in itself, however, also conveys certain information: it strongly influences the perception of the store as well as indicating its target customers and the range of services offered. This information is contained in the following aspects of the product assortment:

► Type of products sold – a delicatessen as well as a shop selling jewellery or fur coats is more likely to be associated with luxury and sophisticated service than a shop which sells stationery or household chemicals.

► Dimensions: the width (the number of product groups) and the depth (the number of products within each group). A wide and deep assortment signifies an opportunity for comprehensive shopping according to the 'everything under one roof' formula. Shoppers, however, may be concerned that it also means a time-consuming shopping process and thus consider such a store inappropriate for daily or even frequent shopping. A very deep assortment is a prerequisite for building and consolidating the position and image of a specialised retail establishment, which customers will be willing to visit even if it involves travelling a considerable distance.

► Selection of brands, including own brands. A shop offering goods from the economy and 'value for money' categories cannot attain the image of a luxury store, which may be necessary in order to attract the desired category of buyers. Introducing premium brands to the product assortment can upgrade the image of, for example, a discount store. Promoting country of origin can affect customers, too (Kubeláková and Košičiarová,

2016). An important role in terms of communication is played by the attributes of own-label products: the type of goods (basic necessities or products meeting higher level needs), their prices and packaging. They can contribute to creating the image of a retailer with an exclusive offering, or have the opposite effect.

5.3.2 Price and price tags

The price is not only the fundamental tool for creating revenue, but also a means of communicating the concept behind a retailer's business operations. Low prices mean that the offering is affordable and addressed to a wide range of buyers, but it may also suggest inferior quality. For example, discount stores build their market position on a low-price strategy, which is possible because of the low prices they pay to suppliers and the low cost of maintaining stores (fast product turnover, small number of staff, unsophisticated interior, low-cost location). Thus, in this case low quality concerns the service rather than the products. Customers, especially those from the smart shoppers group, expect such solutions. Hence the view that these shops have transformed from 'crisis shops' into 'rational shops' (Domański, 2005). However, very low prices, particularly when combined with a large proportion of own brands, may result in feelings of increased risk associated with making purchases. On the other hand, high prices, connected with the high quality of goods and service, lend credibility to a quality assessment. Additionally, they contribute to customer selection, which may be desirable in the retail trade. However, if the price level does not correspond to the market potential, the effect of a high-price policy will be negative. In the retail sector, because of the extensive range of products amounting to tens of thousands of items, it is possible to diversify the level of prices and margins for individual products. This means that the prices of some (relatively few) goods may be low (with low margins), whereas the prices of other products may be considerably higher (with higher margins). This may favourably affect the retailer's image: the customers perceive the price level as low, while the retailer has a high profit margin.

Communication is conveyed not only through the price level, but also through the manner in which the items are displayed. Discrete price labels are used primarily in the case of luxury goods, and the message they communicate is that the price does not matter, which may result in the customer being ashamed to check the price. In the case of special offers, for example on promotional stands, the price is of paramount importance: it is the main means of attracting customers' attention and so it must be suitably large and clear. Additional communicative functions can be fulfilled by a price tag containing information on the price of a given item as well as the price per unit of weight or volume of the product. Because in most cases a larger package means a lower unit price, this practice encourages customers to buy larger quantities of goods.

5.3.3 In-store promotion-mix

Out of all the instruments belonging to retailers' promotion-mix, the majority (sales promotions, some forms of advertising and personal selling) can be used in the store. While advertising in classic media is becoming less effective, communication through stores reaches the consumer at a place and time where most purchase decisions are made (Gedenk *et al.*, 2006). Promotion instruments used as part of in-store communication are based on direct messages, the content of which is verbalized and addressed directly to consumers.

5.3.4 Sales promotions

Sales promotions play an important role in the marketing programme of retailers. Instruments for sales promotion are intended to temporarily increase the attractiveness of an offer based on the price, the aim of which is to encourage customers to make immediate buying decisions. Such offers are usually combined with special displays (organized in a dedicated place in a block form). In each such case, the customer receives a message: buy now. This message can be implemented in different ways:
- a temporary reduction in the price of a product, displayed next to the earlier higher price;
- two products for the price of one;
- reduced price on the basis of discount coupons;
- including free gifts;
- including free product samples;
- stamps given to customers after making purchases, which can be exchanged for premiums.

5.3.5 In-store advertising

In-store communication makes use of selected forms of advertising: printed (leaflets, posters), audio (audio advertising spots), and audio-visual (advertising spots broadcast on in-store monitors). As mentioned earlier, these types of materials are prepared either by manufacturers (this is the most common practice) or by retailers. They have the following aims:
- to inform customers about new products;
- to remind customers about existing products;
- to encourage customers to buy.

All forms of advertising are tools of direct communication. Their effectiveness can be significantly increased through personalizing the message, which means addressing different offers to customers with specific characteristics; for example age, gender, purchase history, etc. This can be implemented through a system of digital signage, in which the advertising message displayed on the monitor is adjusted to the age and gender of the person who is standing in front of it (Borusiak and Pierański, 2015).

5.3.6 Personal selling

Personal selling is the oldest form of in-store communication and generally of retailers' communication. Due to the high cost connected with communicating the message to a single buyer, it applies to expensive unsought products. The effectiveness of personal selling is very high. The mechanisms for its impact are based on all the attributes of interpersonal communication: the ability to determine the needs of a particular buyer; customizing the communication; interaction, intended to dispel the customer's doubts; as well as the ability to persuade.

5.4 Visual merchandising techniques

Visual merchandising is a term frequently used in the context of in-store marketing[1]. It refers to the way products are presented in a retail outlet in a broad sense, including the overall store design, store layout and other aspects of the store environment (Zentes *et al.*, 2007). All these elements combine to create an important component of the company's communication policy as they are capable of influencing the behaviour of consumers, who are often completely unaware of this influence. With the help of visual merchandising, both quantitative and qualitative objectives can be achieved: retailers can increase the level of sales (especially through an increase in impulse purchases); achieve the desired structure of sales (due to a better presentation of high-margin products); and enhance their image. The following techniques are particularly important for achieving these objectives:

5.4.1 Store traffic manipulation

The necessity to control the movement of customers in a store is primarily connected with the significant differences in the productivity of different store parts. Generally speaking, the locations close to the entrance of a shop have a higher productivity than places at the back of the store (Underhill, 2001). The control of customer traffic is intended to activate the low-productivity areas. This can be achieved in two ways:

Controlling customer traffic through the store layout, which involves creating a maze (through the appropriate arrangement of the fixtures, but also, for example, erecting partitions), in which the shopper moves methodically around the entire shop; this system is sometimes also called the race track layout (Sullivan and Adcock, 2003). This method,

---

[1] Less frequently, the term 'merchandising' is used to describe such activities (Buttle, 1984; Borusiak, 2009).

although usually effective, may result in the shoppers feeling pressurised to move according to a certain pattern and forced to spend a large amount of time in the store. Thus, it may deter them from paying frequent visits to the shop.

Controlling the customer traffic through an alternating arrangement of goods bought on impulse and the so-called magnet products (those that the customers have planned to buy). Most commonly, the former are placed in the so-called 'good places' and the latter in worse places. Creating a 'slalom' between the different groups of products is a prerequisite for the success of this method. The message conveyed to the customers by means of this method lacks an element of strong pressure; instead, it contains a suggestion of arbitrariness in choosing the path along which customers move around the store. Thus, the store can be perceived as appropriate for frequent shopping.

In order to implement these methods, the following tools are used:
▸ background music;
▸ arrangement of the sales area;
▸ lighting.

With the help of music it is possible to control the speed with which customers walk around the store, affect their emotions, create preferences for specific products, and consequently influence the sales. Music can also favourably affect the well-being of the employees and increase their productivity. It is difficult to precisely determine the extent to which shoppers are aware of the music broadcast in stores; it is possible that its influence on customer behaviour is subconscious (Milliman, 1982), which means that the impact of music on the behaviour of shoppers may be tested with the help of neuromarketing methods.

The second element for managing customer traffic is the way in which the store space is arranged, which determines the paths that customers will follow. Different configurations in terms of these space arrangements correspond to the two methods for controlling customer traffic described above.

The intensity, colour and type of lighting also have an impact on customer behaviour: spotlights can attract attention to certain groups of products, and lighting of a specific colour can make products look more attractive (Berčík *et al.*, 2015). This issue is also the subject of neuromarketing research and will be considered in the next chapter.

5.4.2 Store layout

The store layout is related to the adopted method of controlling the flow of customer traffic. Generally, there are three basic types of layout: grid, free-flow and boutique. The main feature of the grid layout is arranging the counters and fixtures in long rows, which, apart from the ones by the walls, are set parallel to each other. The grid system is the most widely used in large stores (discount stores, supermarkets, sometimes hypermarkets), but also in smaller shops which sell fast moving goods. A store organised in this way creates the impression of a warehouse and limits the customers' ability to move freely around the sales area. The grid layout creates an image appropriate for a store offering products at low prices.

The free-flow layout involves placing individual display equipment (usually tables, racks, baskets) around the sales floor. This is used for the sale of articles in the shopping goods category; for example clothing, footwear or sporting goods in such types of stores as specialty stores and department stores. The free-flow system offers considerable freedom in terms of designing the store interior. The customer is free to choose their path around the store. The interior of a store arranged in this way creates an atmosphere of relaxation and lack of pressure.

The last of the basic systems is the boutique layout, which consists in creating separate, specialized stands around the sales floor. This concept is consistent with the spirit of category management, which is based on building a product assortment around specific groups of needs. This layout gives the shoppers a sense of freedom of movement, and at the same time, by displaying categories of complementary products, helps customers become acquainted with the store's offering.

5.4.3 Product allocation

The manner of allocating space to goods both in the entire store and within the individual planograms communicates a great deal of indirect information based on image and associations. A supermarket in which fresh product is placed in the entrance area is more likely to be seen as appropriate for everyday shopping than a supermarket where customers encounter household chemicals immediately after entering the store. The perceived high quality of fresh produce close to the entrance can also, through the halo effect, be transferred to other goods on offer. Another aspect of the communicative effect regarding the placement of products is the way in which products are grouped. Grouping according to comprehensive needs (e.g. all cleaning products in one place) or target groups (e.g. all products for children, including food, hygiene, cosmetics, toys, etc.) makes the system clearer for customers than grouping according to the branch of industry (i.e. the similarity of components). Finally, there is the arrangement of products within a planogram: decisions about allocating specific goods to specific shelves and the number of the so-called facings communicates information relating to the completeness of the offering, the ease of finding specific products, and the quality of the entire product assortment.

5.4.4 Ambient techniques: lighting, colours, music, scent, temperature

Apart from the previously mentioned elements, a store environment also consists of such design features as the colour scheme, smell and temperature. Importantly, the sensory experiences that result from the impact of ambient techniques affect consumers on different levels: both the conscious and unconscious. As a result, communication is transferred to the behavioural, emotional and symbolic levels; and each of the elements involved can exert a strong influence, both positive and negative, on the moods and emotions of customers. The sense of smell is the most direct of the senses, because the signal (i.e. the smell) basically does not change on the way to the brain. A smell may encourage shoppers to buy certain products, but it can also build certain associations. In turn, sight is generally considered to be the most powerful of the human senses because it is to the greatest extent responsible for gathering information about the environment. The impact of visual messages cannot be overestimated. Finally, the sense of hearing is always active and cannot be turned off. Music can influence both conscious and unconscious customer behaviour (Hulten *et al.,* 2011). The ways in which these instruments can exert an influence on buyers are the subject of intensive research (Morrison *et al.,* 2011); they may also be a subject for neuromarketing research.

5.5 New trends in in-store communication

A number of innovative solutions continue to appear in the area of in-store communication. For many of them, the common denominator is the personalization of communication. These include the following:
▶   Solutions for customer recognition: technologies for recognising customers directly through facial recognition, and recognition technologies which use applications installed in mobile devices – smartphones or tablets (Borusiak and Pierański, 2013).
▶   Big data systems, which make it possible to create customer profiles based on information from multiple sources (directly observable data, such as gender and approximate age; data obtained from the Internet, both behavioural and declarative; data from the retailer's IT system relating to a given client).
▶   Technologies for transferring personalized messages, i.e. digital signage and applications for mobile devices (smartphones and tablets).

Personalization of in-store advertising is such an innovative solution that its effectiveness is still inadequately researched. On the one hand, customers tend to assess personalized advertising as better (Fiorletta, 2013), on the other – it causes controversy as it is connected with violating the privacy of customers (Pope and Lowen, 2009). There is no doubt, however, that very dynamic developments can be observed nowadays regarding solutions aimed at personalizing communication with customers.

5.6 Web 2.0 and its possibilities in communication with the customer

If consumers have a free decision about their choice by buying products or making demands on services or if these decisions are manipulated by producers or big companies was inexplicit for a long time. But it is clear that companies itself are not totally committed to the influences of the market but influence the market itself. (Logstrup and Logstrup, 1989).

The internet has recovered from the new economy crisis in 2000 and changed and developed fundamentally. The new so called Web 2.0 is characterised by easier possibilities to communicate or provide information without having an IT degree. So, all persons now can use the internet as active users. It changed from a passive to an active mass media. (Heiden, 2014) The ways of communication an articulation can be text (posts, comments, ratings,...), pictures, sound and video. Especially social networks make it easy to satisfy users' needs of communication and interaction.

Contrary to the prevailing feeling of anonymity when using the internet, the opposite is usually the case. Every click, every visited page, every sold or not sold item and nowadays even dwell time on pages, subpages and posts and even mouse gestures are saved and analysed anonymous but also user related. On the one hand data recordings can happen directly on the terminal of the user e.g. in the form of cookies. On the other hand tracking and tracing is possible online by page integrated software. Both ways mostly are invisible to the user. Companies of this tracking software are acting comprehensive. They use the collected data to be in the position to react targeted on other places in the net. Just using the internet makes everyone to a 'glass costumer' with all of his preferences, aversions and primarily his needs. Companies are using their knowledge for individually targeted manipulation of the consumers' behaviour of every single user. According to a scientific study only a few 'Likes' in a social network are necessary to figure out precisely the preferences of the users. Furthermore a classification in ethnic origin, religion, sex and sexual orientation is possible. (Kosinski *et al.*, 2013)

5.7 Influencing online purchase decisions and how to handle the modern web

To influence customers' behaviour it is important to understand how a consumer makes a buying decision. Basically the buying process can be divided in three main phases: the time before, during and after the purchase. The first phase again is subdivided in awareness phase, consideration phase and decisions phase. In all stages of the buying process consumers can be manipulated selectively. (Comegys *et al.,* 2006)

To wake the need for a product or a service to a customer, the absence of it must be aware first or must be made aware. Conventional advertisement mainly is used to initiate the awareness phase by trying to show up a potential need. It does not matter if the need really exists or not. If the costumer is interested in any way a conscious or subconscious reaction comes about. If not, the costumer is not interested. Based on the collected data of the costumers online behaviour companies nowadays are in the position to previously know which product most likely is interesting for the user. Social networks also use the data to place ads of their clients precisely. Online traders also respond to the buying habits of their clients and show products on their landing pages which fit individually to the purchase behaviour. Special apps for mobile devices are able to collect personalised data even more precisely. Here also the localisation of the exact position of device can be a precondition to use the app. Mobile apps additionally prevent the mixture of more than one user in a household. Also joint data of online behaviour connected with the personal profile may lead to buy recommendations. One step further goes the online trader *amazon*. The company had been granted a patent which was applied with the intention to supply the costumer with goods before the costumer even clicked the 'Purchase' button. Basis for it are collected data of the purchase behaviour (Bensinger, 2014). The current slogan of *amazon*'s new mobile app is 'Thought it. Bought it.'

The search phase starts if a customer has decided to buy a product or to hire a service. Search engines, special comparison portals and online marketplaces have been developed over the past years to make a search for products as easy as possible. The following consideration phase and decisions phase are supported by providing properties, prices, origin and other information about the desired product and similar products. Product ratings from other customers nowadays are of decisive importance in this phase. 80% of the online shoppers think it is important that a product has a good or very good rating. (TNS Infratest GmbH, 2012). The presentation of alternatives to the searched product in this stage is used to eventually move the purchase decision at the last moment, possibly to a product of better quality or higher value. But also cheaper alternatives are presented, if the desired item actually is too expensive for the customer and to prevent an abort. Online traders for example present products which other customer how bought the desired product also were interested in.

During the purchase phase, what means the short moment of buying a product and after the purchase decision finally is completed, the online traders again try to manipulate the customers. Now they try to sell some supplies. The argumentation is: 'Other clients how bought this product, also bought that one.' or 'This product usually is bought together with that product.' The aim is to gain an impulsive buying decision, what mostly is spontaneous and imprudent (Heiden, 2014). What additional products are presented normally is not a direct decision of the online trader, but it is based on analytics of customers' purchase and behaviour data.

By succeeding the purchase the post-purchase phase starts, because after the purchase is before the purchase. The client now can follow one's need for communication. The preparation of a positive rating connects the client more to the product and may lead to a later purchase of the same product or a product of the same brand. Other clients rely to positive ratings. They provide the feeling of buying a useful product.

All technical possibilities are used nowadays to push customers more and more targeted to a purchase decision and it becomes more difficult to defend against surveillance over the internet. By using the internet with a browser it is possible to install additional programs to prevent collection personalised data about user's behaviour. It could also be meaningful to logout from internet services after use, because sites are in the position to be active in the background and follow the user's actions. Some also browsers provide a 'private surf modus'. It is also feasible to block advertisement as far as possible by using special software.

By using mobile apps it can be hard or even impossible to change or stop transmitting of data. To agree the terms is required to actually be able to use the app. Which information is transmitted or analysed is unclear for the user.

To not be committed to the companies for the individual user it is necessary to be conscious that one's online behaviour can be followed at any time and it will be used for commercial purposes and other thinks. A regulation of this practice by the government is usually difficult and need years. If consumers have a free decision about their choice by buying products or making demands on services or if these decisions are manipulated by producers or big companies is today and in the future up to the customers and their behaviour.

References

Bensinger, G., 2014. Amazon wants to ship your package before you buy it. Wall Street Journal. Available at: http://tinyurl.com/mwzab7b.

Berčík, J., Horská, E., Wang, W.Y. and Chen, Y.C., 2015. How can food retailing benefit from neuromarketing research: a case of various parameters of store illumination and consumer response. 143rd Joint EAAE/AAEA Seminar, March 25-27, 2015, Naples, Italy.

Borusiak, B., 2009. Merchandising. Wydawnictwo Uniwersytetu Ekonomicznego w Poznaniu, Poznań, Poland.

Borusiak, B. and Pierański, B., 2013. Nowoczesne narzędzia w komunikacji marketingowej przedsiębiorstw handlowych. Handel wewnętrzny w Polsce 2009-2014.

Borusiak, B. and Pierański, B., 2015. Możliwości personalizacji oferty w przedsiębiorstwach handlu detalicznego. Handel wewnętrzny w Polsce 2010-2015.

Buttle, F., 1984. Merchandising. European Journal of Marketing 18(6-7): 104-124.

Comegys, C., Hannula, M. and Väisänen, J., 2006. Longitudinal comparison of Finnish and US online shopping behaviour among university students. The five-stage buying decision process. Journal of Targeting, Measurement and Analysis for Marketing 14: 336-356.

Domański T., 2005. Strategie rozwoju handlu. PWE, Warszawa, Poland.

Fiorletta A., 2013. Personalized marketing improves brand perception. Available at: http://tinyurl.com/moov7x3.

Gedenk, K., Neslin, S.A. and Ailawadi, K.L., 2006. Sales promotion. In: Krafft, M. and Mantrala, M.K. (eds.) Retailing in the 21st century. Current and Future Trends. Springer, Berlin, Germany.

Gilbert, D., 1999. Retail marketing management. Prentice Hall, Edinburgh, UK.

Heiden, K., 2014. Kaufverhalten im Web 2.0. Der Einfluss von Bewertungen auf Kaufentscheidungen. BSc-thesis, Hochschule für Wirtschaft und Recht Berlin, Berlin, Germany.

Hulten, B., Broweus, N. and Van Dijk, M., 2011. Marketing sensoryczny. PWE, Warszawa, Poland.

Kosinski, M., Stillwell, D. and Graepel, T., 2013. Private traits and attributes are predictable from digital records of human behavior. Proceedings of the National Academy of Sciences of the USA 110: 5802-5805.

Kubelaková, A.-K.I., 2016. Organic food and its position in retail stores in Slovak Republic. In: The agri-food value chain: challenges for natural resources management and society, International Scientific Days 2016, May 19-20, 2016, Nitra, Slovak Republic, pp. 1036-1042.

Logstrup, K.E. and Logstrup, R., 1989. Norm und Spontanität. Ethik und Politik zwischen Technik und Dilettantokratie. Tübingen, Mohr, Tübingen, Germany, 278 pp.

Milliman R.E., 1982. Using background music to affect The Behavior of Supermarket Shoppers. Journal of Marketing 46: 86-87.

Morrison, M. Gan, S. Dubelaar, C. and Oppewal, H., 2011. In-store music and aroma influences on shopper behavior and satisfaction. Journal of Business Research 64: 558-564.

Pope, J.A. and Lowen, A.M., 2009. Marketing implications of privacy concerns in the US and Canada. Direct Marketing 3(4): 301-326.

Sullivan, M. and Adcock, D., 2003. Marketing w handlu detalicznym. Oficyna Ekonomiczna, Kraków, Poland.

TNS Infratest GmbH, 2012. Vertrauen beim Online-Einkauf. Eine Sonderstudie im Rahmen des (N)ONLINER Atlas 2012. Available at: http://tinyurl.com/lvrlqe3.

Underhill, P., 2001. Dlaczego kupujemy. MT Biznes, Warszawa, Poland.

Zentes, J., Morschett, D. and Schramm-Klein, H., 2007. Strategic retail management. Gabler, Wiesbaden, Germany.

6. Application of neuromarketing in retailing and merchandising

Ľ. Nagyová*, E. Horská and J. Berčík

Slovak University of Agriculture in Nitra, Faculty of Economics and Management, Department of Marketing and Trade, Tr. A. Hlinku 2, 949 76 Nitra, Slovak Republic; ludmila.nagyova@uniag.sk

Abstract

Impact of all brands, products, advertisements and merchandising tools used as a part of in-store communication act together at the point of sale during shopping. The subject of marketers' and researchers' interest is the measurement of the final purchasing interest and observation of consumer behaviour at the point of sale – what, where, when, why and for how much are consumers buying. However, there are a high number of measurable variables, such as perceived simplicity of finding out the products, overall impression of the shop and likelihood of return, consumer behaviour is the final subject of interest. This simple fact widely influences the possibilities of the most effective application of neuromarketing methods used for the measurement of shopping experiences. To show the alternatives of using various merchandising tools and consequently neuromarketing methods to measure their impact on consumer behaviour, is shown in the chapter.

Keywords: neuromarketing, retailing, merchandising, customer

Learning objectives

After studying this chapter you should be able to:
- Apply various merchandising tools in retailing
- Decide on neuromarketing methods, techniques, research plans and objectives to measure the impact of merchandising and in-store conditions on buying behaviour and decision to do purchase

Elena Horská and Jakub Berčík (eds.) **Neuromarketing in food retailing**
DOI 10.3921/978-90-8686-843-8_6, © Wageningen Academic Publishers 2017

6.1 Merchandising in retailing

Merchandising as word originates from English word merchandise, which means commodity/ to trade. It is a department that deals with the marketing care for products mainly in the retail trade. Merchandising encompasses many activities carried out by either manufacturers or retailers, but also advertising agencies. Main objective of these activities is to ensure that the products are available to the customers in the required parameters thus ensuring higher sales and revenues.

> Merchandising is a phenomenon which uses various techniques and methods to make sure that only 'our' product becomes the focus of attention of the consumer. Merchandising is the final and most important step to be taken in order to deliver goods at the right time, price and highest possible quantity to the consumer.
>
> (Kotler and Armstrong, 1992)

The definition of the term merchandising as a way of suitable presentation and product placement falls into the area of corporate marketing. Merchandising has to ensure that the right product will be at the right place at the right time in the right quantity and at the right price. Merchandising can be characterized as a marketing of the point of sale, or as a marketing at the point of sale (Masson and Wellhoff, 1985).

The common and most important for all definitions of merchandising is the aspect of perfect knowledge of the point of sale by the dealers or specialists in merchandising. We cannot forget the fact that the right merchandising always leads to the sale of goods, and if not, it is not the right merchandising.

The beginnings of the application of the principles of merchandising can be seen in the mid of 19th century in connection with the development of self-service. Previously widely used counter sales made it impossible for the customer to get in direct contact with the goods and the main actor of the sale remained the salesman, who stimulated the customer to the purchase of product (primarily by his arguments). Conversely, with the introduction of self-service stores, the product was left on the shelf to sell itself without the involvement of vendors. Another important milestone in the development of merchandising was the end of the 50s of the 20th century, when the first large stores (soon supermarkets, later hypermarket) have appeared. Products began to be placed on shelves together with a large number of competing products, and with that the need to position them to the right place, but also to the suitable arrangement of sales units as well as of shopping environment have increased. Currently, the application of the principles of merchandising is an obvious necessity for large stores primarily in food selling, but its application is continually expanding into many other types of stores. Merchandising is 'forcing' people to consume more by creating the desire to buy. Some see in merchandising, in addition to the teaching about the arrangement of goods in the sale areas, also the activities for the care of point of sales (including trained staff) and promotion (special stands, tastings, etc.) – Bechiňová, 2010.

By the effect of the concentration of retail capacity and the internationalization of markets, the existing trading companies search for the system of business operations, that would enable them to adapt the offer and forms of sale to the constantly changing expectations of buyers, in order to ensure the sustainable development. Consumers are increasingly informed and before they show their interest in a product, they require the traders to run retail units in terms of their requirements. The principles of current merchandising, as one of the most important tools of communication mix of the retailer associated with the store, correspond to these requirements (Kita, 2011).

The retail unit is made up of system components, which include:
► the goods;
► retail activities;
► mechanization and organizational means and equipment.

According to Starzyczná (2001), the other components of the retail unit are:
► sales area;
► workers;
► construction and technical layout of operating units, to which can be allocated also the legislative, financial and communication elements associated with the sales.

Prážská and Jindra (2006) characterized retail unit as an integral part of the logistic movement of goods from the producer to the consumer. The object of the retail unit is:
► the goods which has several forms – such as the goods themselves, as range, as supply and as technology group;
► and movement of goods, ensured by the activities performed by the employees with the use of organizational resources and facilities, while the level of commercial and operational activities is a demonstration of the know-how, processes, skills and management of people in the retail unit.

For this reason, they characterized the retail unit as a system made up of these elements and their inter-linkages and determining the nature of the retail unit is the goods. Their presentation in modern operating units of the retail with self-service cannot be left to the chance. On the contrary, in these stores the clients communicate mainly with the goods and therefore it should not be unnoticed by the consumer. As the number of sales staff in supermarkets and hypermarkets is declining, thereby to the forefront comes the merchandising, which has to ensure the achievement of the highest retail sales based on the optimal use of the sales area.

Viestová (2008) defines the retail unit as:

> The store, where the movement of goods has been completed by the sales to the consumer. The sale becomes more perfect based on the knowledge of consumer needs, which enable that the retailers become marketers and merchandisers. Retailer acts as a purchaser, who gets out from the needs and expectations of consumers in the direction of the sales marketing concept, which enables him to achieve high productivity and profitability with the use of customized managing tools of the store. Retailers are thus also becoming the largest users of modern business technologies in order to the better satisfaction of consumer needs.

The retail unit can be defined from the following aspects:
▸ territorial (localization in the defined area);
▸ building (such as room, resp. satellite or multifunctional building);
▸ technical (hardware);
▸ legislative and organizational (part of an organizational structure);
▸ performance and technology (layout of stores, operating time, material liability, etc.);
▸ marketing (the location of the merchandising – the impact of store layout and product presentation on customer behaviour).

The basic dimensions of merchandising at the retail include:
▸ organization of product placement – based on the segmentation of markets and brands with the idea of better understanding of consumers;
▸ management of shelves, brands and segments – based on the management of rack system, assortment, arrangement of shops, good items and prices. The size of rack system (e.g. height 200-220 cm, width 70-100 cm, depth 20-60 cm) as the most prevalent form of product placement depends on the size of retail, width of aisles between the shelves and the turnover of goods;
▸ attraction of the customer's attention – the arrangement of the shelves in the store, brand and the store layout, advertising at the point of sale, accessories, and furniture of the store creates the image and identity of the retail and they have to be attractive to the customers (Kita, 2011).

Based on the given dimensions, the merchandising can be divided into:

▶ Organizing merchandising focused on the layout of goods – deals with the deployment of goods in stores in order to get the highest sales and so that his layout should met the expectations of its customers – how to deploy the exhibition equipment of the shop, where to place the goods in the store, how to place the goods (by brand or DPT), what should be the follow-up assortment of goods, at which level of the exhibition equipment to place the goods.

▶ Merchandising focused on the management of the retail range – the layout of exhibition equipment which determines the perception of the retail's offer to the customers, the nature and amount of purchase. Attention is drawn to the location of the entrance to the store and its total construction orientation (transitions between shelves, departments, aisles, etc.).

▶ Merchandising focused on catching the customer's attention with the aim of customer's help to find a product as quickly as possible, to stimulate the interest in the purchase and remove barriers to the purchase process. The sophisticated harmony of colours, the logic of processions through the store, lighting, showcases with the proposed products, music and other support the impulsive purchase and emphasize the aesthetic and cultural side of business (Sloboda and Richterová, 1988). The total interior of the shop should be in accordance with the storefront. Some international retails have drawn up specific documents in the form of manuals relating to merchandising, which are updated every time a new product gets to the market.

The current trends in merchandising focused on catching the customer's attention are concerned about:

▶ Return to the colour scheme in order that the shops will feel optimistic based on the use of bright colours. The use of colours can also help to split the sales area.

▶ Use of visual aids relying on new technologies, respectively traditional media such as dummy allowing the presentation of the new collection of goods, etc.; – lighting and lighting effects complement the colour solution of the store. Lighting helps to the modification of cold zones and points out the offered product. A well-lit room is an additional increase in sales volume.

▶ Manners of presentation:
  • stepped pattern creates the effect of floors;
  • fan-shaped pattern uses the most interesting type of goods to draw the customer's attention;
  • pyramidal pattern is used for the display of more goods on a relatively small area;
  • winding pattern is characterized by its informal balance.

▸ The equipment of the store can in addition to white-sided, respectively double sided shelves of wood, glass, metal, etc. be from a different material, confirming the identity of the label.
▸ Respect for the environment remains a major source of inspiration for current and future trends in the attraction of customer's attention.

6.2 Visual merchandising in retailing

Merchandising in sales units is closely related to the other two types of merchandising – *visual merchandising* and *sensory merchandising*. Also it is considered as a part of in-store communication as it is described in Chapter 5 (Borusiak *et al.*, 2017).

Practical implication 1:

Potential customer has his first contact with the business place while moving by the point of sale or its store window. It takes 3-7 seconds for the showcase to intrigue him. In the present, the businessman must display in the store window such products which attract people to the extent that they desire to enter the store. Store window is also the place where the seller informs the customer about discounts and promotions that can be found in the store.

If the customer steps over the shop threshold, it still does not mean that they buy anything. Customer has to choose the product and then to buy it and that might be a long way to go. Upon entering the shop customer starts to investigate what's around and if it is worth to continue with exploring the store. Therefore, it is necessary at the entrance of the store to sell such goods, which are new, discounted or strategic, those are the ones that deliver the highest sales margin.

Customer must feel comfortable in the store. If this happens, he then returns and buys again. To make customer feel good, it is necessary to ensure the correct arrangement of shelves, displayed goods and background music.

Exhibited goods must be located at eye level of the customer we wish to purchase the goods. For adults the shelves with products should be located at a height of 150 cm from the floor, but not more than 190 cm. These dimensions present the most common visual field, that's why there should be located such goods on which vendors have the largest sales margin. It is important to pay attention also to organization inside the store, which should be systematic and mainly transparent.

For the store is also important well-chosen lighting and music. Brighter lights better illuminate individual products, showing off their colours. Good handling of lights will highlight the colour of products. Music can increase customer's interest to buy more too. Promotion in the store should engage customer.

Cashiers are the most important place in the store. If customer wants to buy something, he must know immediately where to aim to pay for it. Unclear checkout and confused customers will lead eventually to lost sale. Payment should take place quickly and easily. If it is held up, customer then might not visit the store next time. It is also important to avoid the long lines at the cashiers (based on http://franchising.sk/abc-firma/1771/prilakaj-zakaznika/).

Visual merchandising represents the higher merchandising category and deals with matters related to product showcasing in detail while applying such methods and hiring such personnel which bring merchandising to an almost artistic level. According to Morgan (2011), the task of a visual merchandiser is to create such an in-store environment and ambience that allows the customer to identify with company business image. Bell and Ternus (2006) state that visual merchandiser should think under the SCAMPER model (a tool for generating of unusual solutions): Substitute + Combine + Adapt + Modify (minify, magnify) + Put to other users + Reverse (rearrange).

Visual merchandising represents all that the customer perceives with his own senses (Horská *et al.*, 2010). First of all, it is a tool of achieving the target sale on sales area and also a mechanism communicating with customers and influencing their buying decision (Bhalli, 2010). Visual merchandising is an independent component of communication providing customers with information on what the store may offer. This term is often associated with work clothes of employees and storefronts, but in fact it has tools to make the sales area more charming and attractive for customers (Pegler, 2011).

As stated by Horská *et al.* (2014), in addition to the merchandising tools, the concept of visual merchandising includes also the elements of in-store communication and retailing marketing (Figure 6.1). It is necessary to understand the term merchandising, which means to support the sale of certain commodities. In other words, visual merchandising could be defined as a process that supports the product sales with creating the images in mind giving the customer an idea to make a purchase (Bell and Ternus, 2006). Another definition by Diamond and Diamond (2010) says, it is an effective way of the exposed products' presentation leading to the customer's increased interest in the product and influencing the customer's purchasing behaviour in favour of the merchant.

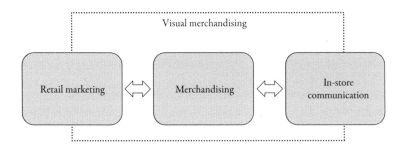

Figure 6.1. Components of visual merchandising (Horská *et al.,* 2014).

According to Horská, *et al.* (2011), visual merchandising deals with increasing sales using the effect of the shop's design. Its main principle is the interest to increase sales through the art of design. It can be implemented as follows:

▸ exposure of products in the most beautiful light;
▸ communication with customer;
▸ act in a customer-friendly way in order to make a customer buy the product/service;
▸ present the product from the customer's perspective;
▸ reduce disturbances in the shop.

Multi-sensorial stimulation, as a part of visual merchandising, is crucial for ensuring the favourable purchasing atmosphere and welfare of customers in the sales area. The term 'atmosphere' itself reflects an influence of sensorial stimuli from environment, such as sight, hearing, smell and touch on consumer behaviour (Kotler, 1973/1974). It consists of helpful elements affecting an individuals' positive side, such as exterior, shop's interior arrangement, product display and interior, within which act light, colours, music, air quality and scents (Figure 6.2).

6.3 Sensory merchandising in retailing

Sensory merchandising can be defined as:

> A new form of marketing in retail using such factors that create an environment and atmosphere in the shop (music, aroma, colour, taste and tactile elements); causing consumers to respond positively to the purchase of certain goods.
>
> (www.popai.cz/lexikon-vyrazu/index.php?id=90)

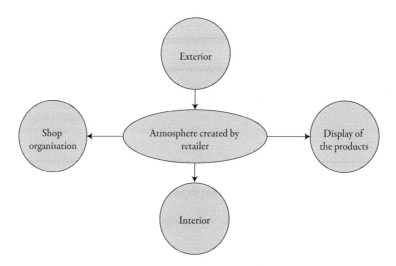

Figure 6.2. Elements of visual merchandising (based on Singh *et al.,* 2015).

Sensory merchandising is analysing how customers respond to the physical retail shop environment and how they adjust to it. Retailers are trying more and more to impact customer senses to offer each customer genuine experiences, entertainment and distraction. The elements of sensory merchandising include lighting, retail shop interior colour design, background sound / music, aroma and microclimate conditions.

6.3.1 Lighting inside the store

Through specific visual elements we can create attractive environment and intentionally guide customer's attention to those products which we want him to notice. High quality lighting improves the image of retail chains, attracts potential customers, focuses their attention to offered products and ultimately increases sale. Characteristics of lighting used in grocery stores may be designed in different ways, and this way contributing to the created impression of visual quality of the shop as a whole, but on the other hand, may be used also to cover the low quality of offered products.

This is the case of so called stimulation of the customer, which is running beneath customer's consciousness. Customer thus perceives some light or other stimuli subliminally, i.e. without being noticed (Schiffman and Kanuk, 2004). Warren (2005) states that modern customer perceives colours, in particular earthy, glossy and wood colours. Another important factor is also the way of how the colours are illuminated.

Consistent design of the retail store helps the company to create unified/uniformed image (Kelly, 1952). Bosch *et al.* (2005) agree and declare that the lighting is even able to create identity of trademark.

Custers *et al.* (2010) offer recommendations for lighting of the retail store: interesting lighting of shop façade, attractive lighting of store window, dynamic and unusual lighting of products. These recommendations are going beyond the conventional retail store presentation and help to create an interesting company identity. Authors mention also the solution for overall illumination of the retail store: it is advisable to choose the lighting that brings cosy and lively feeling at the same time. Flynn (1977) remarked that illuminated spaces appear to be brighter and more spacious than dark ones. It is experimentally proved that there exists a positive relationship between brightness and feeling of joy (Zielke and Shielke, 2011). More brightly illuminated products seem to be more attractive for customers and high brightness is even associated with lower price and higher quality (Keavaney and Hunt, 1992). As stated by Karlen and Benya (2011), many people consider illumination the most important factor for attracting the human sight, because up to one quarter of human brain (much more than any other sense) is involved in visual processing. Eyes collecting light and improving focus account for about 70% of sensory receptors. However, the brain itself assigns a sense to colours, shapes, facial expressions and landscapes as they are seen (Pradeep, 2010).

Lighting is used not only for accented lighting of food products, but also to induce photometric reactions in food products being sold.

Practical implication 2

The lighting in the sales unit incorporates the total sales area lighting, as well as the lighting of individual racks, signs and lighting targeted on specific goods. The choice of lighting fixtures should match to the size of sales unit, the overall style of retail and equipment. Specially selected type of lighting can emphasize the store's image. The main characteristics of lighting levels are the intensity, uniformity, glare and shading. In terms of the intensity, it is important that the store is not in twilight or blasted. This is especially true in the clothes stores, as the incorrectly chosen intensity of the lighting can negatively affect the appearance of the clothing. On the other hand, the brightness can be used to highlight the selected goods (attention must be brought to the lighted product, not the source of light). Suitable lighting is required in all the areas where the customers try or closely inspect the goods (fitting room). In addition to the characteristics of light levels is also essential the colour of the light, which should reflect the overall colour scheme of the interior of the retail unit and respect the assortment focus of the store. The colour of the light affects the appearance of the product and therefore it should be chosen carefully to avoid the distortion of the characteristics of the goods. In the case of clothes stores, it should be ideal if the customers could see the goods directly in the daylight (Bechiňová, 2010).

6.3.2 Colour

Colour is the result of our brain activity and construct of our mind.

(Šikl, 2012)

We consider colours a natural part of our vision of the world, they are the result of electromagnetic waves with different wavelengths.

(Vysekalová, 2012)

Colours attract attention, bring displayed objects closer to reality and can be used to identify and label advertised object .

(Vysekalová, 2012)

Colour is a powerful tool that not only enhances shop atmosphere, but also gives customer a certain mood. People subjectively prefer colours according to gender, age, nationality, religion, and cultural background, political or social affiliation. Colour perception is affected by living conditions and culture.

People not only perceive colours in a certain way, but vice-versa the colours somehow affect humans too (Dannhoferová, 2012). Experts distinguish four ways of colour influence:
1. Physical effect of colour – lies in the visible part of the electromagnetic spectrum, which includes various kinds of light beams, but also, for example, to varying degrees reflectance of surfaces (e.g. light areas reflect more light and dark surfaces absorb more of it).
2. Physiological effect of colour – is based on the effect of light on the human body, especially the human eyes and brain, but also on other anatomical features (e.g. contrasting colours can produce post (negative) after-images, colours also affect our autonomic system).
3. Psychological effect of colour – is based on the effects of colours on our psyche, includes various associations, symbolism, synthesis and stimulation induced in people by colours (e.g. warm colours are more active and act excitingly, while cool colours are mostly soothing).
4. Visual effect of colour – is determined by how the colours manifest the area or space (e.g. warm colours tend to stand out from the picture and on the contrary cool colours usually recede into the background).

Sometimes there's mentioned associative impact of the colours (e.g. red is usually associated with blood, yellow with the sun, green with nature, blue with water, pink acts sweetly, white is pure, etc.). Associative impact of colours is a special case of psychological effect of colours.

Each colour has certain psychological content that depends on one's personality, his qualities, experience and emotional states. It is therefore necessary to analyse not only the general meaning of colour, but also its influence in the context of a given product or service in relation to the characteristics of the target group. Colours are used every day, so it is important to understand their function. Science of colours shows how to work with colours properly.

The main effort of colour theory is to find colour harmony supported by physical, physiological and psychological characteristics of colour perception and bring evidence of basic colour rules that can be applied in practice (Dannhoferová, 2012).

The perception of colour is different in each person and usually changes during their lifetime. It is affected by the cultural environment too. Colour preference based on gender is not that important. Colour associations represent subconscious fusion of colours with different contexts, experiences or objects based on similarities.

We encounter colours in everyday life. They are all around us. For sighted people colours have meaning and are an important psychological tool. Up to 60-80% of visual communication we receive is associated with colours. Colours that surround us affect our subconsciousness. Marketers use colour to broadcast important information, promote the sale and not only attract customers' attention, but transmit a certain message and evoke emotions. People distinguish seven basic spectral colours (Vymětal, 2008):
▸ warm colours – red, orange and yellow;
▸ cold colours – green, blue, indigo and violet.

Warm colours excite us, cold colours are soothing. Kačmařík (2015) divides colours to achromatic (white, black) and chromatic (other colours) (Table 6.1).

Table 6.1. Characteristics of colours.

Colour	Symbolism	Positive emotions	Negative emotions
black	darkness; death	esteem; authority; solemnity; dignity; strength; formality; elegance	destruction; fear; inferiority; solitude; emptiness; sorrow; defiance; protest; negation
white	light; purity; peace; truce	innocence; immaculateness; virtue; faithfulness; sanctity; sterility; perfection; softness; lightness; fragility	coldness; uncertainty; restraint; caution; infinity; sorrow; isolation
grey	neutrality; mediocrity	balance; reliability; modesty; humility; intelligence; dispassionateness	passivity; persistence; disengagement; indecisiveness; uncertainty; capriciousness; sorrow; poverty
yellow	light; sun; gold; spring; youthfulness	pleasure; joyfulness; hope; optimism; wisdom; enlightenment; harmony; intellect; excitability; encouragement; irritation	distrust; jealousy; cautiousness; cowardice; envy; falsity; betrayal
orange	sun; warmth; gold; summer; shimmer	pleasure; joyfulness; amusement; sociability; friendliness; energy; vitality; dynamics; creativity; maturity; harvest; splendour	roughness; whim; defiance
red	blood; fire	love, passion, desire; excitement; vehemence; pride; energy; dynamics; activity; intensity	rebellion; struggle; war; aggression; anger; wrath; cruelty; danger
violet	spirituality; majesty	imagination; mysticism; inspiration; resourcefulness; modesty; humility; wisdom; nobility; dignity	cruelty; suffering; punishment; eccentricity; tension; disquietude; mystery; ignorance; twilight
blue	sky; heavens; air; water; coldness	peace; liberation; righteousness; devotion; trust; silence and tranquillity; rest; relaxation; spirituality; intelligence; discretion; balance	melancholy; submission; lethargy
green	nature; plants; distance; youth; hope; friendship; rebirth	honesty; readiness; promptness; tenacity; perseverance; success; harmony; unity; balance; truth; trust; tranquillity and peace; silence	envy; greediness; inexperience

Practical implication 3

One of the main objectives of the colour design of the interior of the store is to influence the customer's decision making. Therefore, it is suitable to use different colours for various parts of the sales area. For shop windows, entrances and points of sale offering the impulsively purchased goods can be recommended rather warm shade. In the choice of colours is also necessary to take into account the type of the range and its nature, respectively it is possible to incorporate the corporate colours into the interior design of the store. The colour solution of the sales area, it means the colours of the walls, shelves, floors and other presentation devices should not be too pronounced to not attract the customer's attention from the offered goods. Especially the colours should be judiciously chosen in clothes stores, where it is necessary to further harmonize the colours of the walls and furniture with the colours of clothing. It is therefore advisable to choose light pastel or neutral tones that will not interfere with the colouring of the offered goods. Pronounced colour combinations can be used in those places, where the clothes are not directly exposed (e.g. checkout zone, fitting rooms). Some vendors, however, use a sharp colour for the interior to create the store's image (Bechiňová, 2010).

6.3.3 Music and sound amplification in the retail store

Hearing is another sense influencing the emotions. Music therefore represents an inherent element within the tools of visual merchandising. Music can affect not only the time spent in in the store, but also an overall satisfaction of customers at the point of sale. However, it is important to find a compromise within music genres and basic factors of sound amplification, whereas each person perceives music and sound amplification with different sensitivity. Appropriately chosen music and amplification factors bring numerous advantages for retail stores – starting with personnel acting more relaxed and friendly towards customers and ending with encouraged customers spending more time in the shop. From the customer's view, music plays a role while deciding on choice of the store. Last but not least, music can help customers to overcome stress situations (e.g. waiting at the cash desk). Music sufficiently contributes to customer's perception of the environment – whether it is pleasant or unpleasant (Horská et al., 2010). It does not only affect immediate reaction, but it contributes to creation of a long term relationship of customer to given environment. According to Balnar (2008), frequency and intensity (volume) are two most basic characteristics of sound. In the present, various agencies focus on the importance of the psychological influence of music on customers, primarily in retail stores. Music supplements the overall atmosphere of the environment and associated emotional reactions of customers.

It contributes to the customer's opinion whether store environment is perceived as pleasant or unpleasant. It assists in developing long-term customer relationship to the environment. Music creates acoustic background which must conform to the tastes of the target group of customers. It is subjectively influencing the length of time spent by customers in the store when buying products, but also waiting in line at cashiers (Franek, 2002). Correct selection of music can achieve not only that the customers feel comfortable in the environment, but their good impression persists in the subsequent evaluation. Musical preferences depend on age, education, social and economic status in society. Improperly chosen background music can send customer a signal that he found himself in a place where he does not belong. Today's possibilities of recorded music lead to the involuntary listening and this issue is increasingly discussed. Every customer is differently sensitive to surrounding sounds, including the music. This sensitivity is determined by many factors related to hereditary predisposition, one's determination in society, but also listening habits. It is not possible to clearly identify the acoustic background that would be liked by everyone. Due to the prior findings, it is possible to find a compromise ensuring that selected music is not considered tedious by customers less sensitive to surrounding noise and vice versa does not irritate sensitive customers unnecessarily (Mikula, 2015). Music genres, as well as a selection of musical production must respect cultural differences in different countries, because the perception and appreciation may vary (Franek, 2002).

Practical implication 4

Retailers' opinion on music in store:
- 90% recommend other sellers to play music in their stores;
- 76% believe they can positively influence customer behaviour;
- 74% believe that music makes customers happier;
- 73% believe that music will enhance the brand image;
- 63% say that customers spend more time in the store;
- 61% agree that music enhances employee productivity.

Customers' opinion on music in store:
- 84% prefer music over silence;
- 23% would be willing to pay 5% more for the product;
- 45% claim that they would gladly recommend the store to friends and family;
- 55% are more likely to come back again;
- 72% feel that store is more attractive;
- 72% believe that good music will significantly improve store image.

(based on Music Works – Impact of music in retail chains, 2009-2010)

6.3.4 Scent in the shop

Humans have five basic senses. Most of the marketing communication therefore seeks to impress the visual and auditory parts, but aiming to use other human senses too. Suitable fragrance can influence customer's emotions and behaviour, therefore sellers try to attack another one of them – the smell – through aroma marketing (a method of influencing customer behaviour at the sale places with individually selected scent compositions, the art of how to use scent in a marketing campaign and thus influence customer's emotions), which until recently has been underestimated in terms of marketing use.

Marketing and advertising have been historically targeted so that they worked mainly on visual and auditory senses of consumer. Currently, sellers are desperately trying to work on the customer to evoke positive emotions. For sellers, induction of positive emotions in customers increases the chances of selling their products.

The primary interest of sellers is inducing the right atmosphere in the shop so the customer experiences 'awakened desire' to buy something. But, right atmosphere for shopping is not created only by nice-looking store and pleasant and communicative personnel (Štetka, 2012). Among the visual cues also the sensory elements such as music and scents are used in order to keep the customer at the sales area as long as possible.

Becoming ever more important aspect of the right atmosphere is the way of scents and music working in synergy on influencing customer. It is not easy to achieve a harmony between these elements in order to create more pleasant environment and extend customer's time in the shop. Customer feels good in the shop where pleasant scent is consistent with displayed goods. This is a factor perceived mostly at subliminal level. Correctly selected scents can enhance the experience from shopping, but can also act itself as an impulse to start shopping (Alder, 2001).

Use of the smell as part of a marketing campaign brings sellers in addition to acquiring customers another advantage which is more effective brand promotion. Thanks to scent customer creates connection to a particular product, service or brand itself, which leaves in him a lasting memory. This way the brand obtains '3D dimension' because now they can be seen, heard and also felt.

The issue with aroma marketing is that it starts working only after customer walks into the store. It is therefore necessary as soon as possible to attract customer's attention visually – with store appearance. Such methods of positive stimulation of customer directly follow each other, and therefore more and more sellers implement them in their marketing campaigns (Štetka, 2012).

Results of the survey confirmed that 75% of our emotions are generated based on smell and up to 80% of purchase decisions are impulsive. Interesting information is that we remember only 2% of what we hear, only 15% based on taste, but up to 35% of what we smell. Pleasant scent improves our mood up to 40%, can positively influence the desire for specific product and customers are even in such case willing to pay more. As the main advantages of aroma marketing respondents consider that the smell can change the perception of time, increases the emotional bond between customer and product and thereby stimulate the pleasurable effects of shopping, ultimately increasing customer satisfaction.

Practical implication 5

It is scientifically proven that the information perceived by smell affect the decision directly and immediately. Smell is the only one of the senses that cannot be deactivated. With other senses the perception is analysed first, but the scent evokes a feeling or memory immediately. People remember the smell and experience pertaining to it with 65% accuracy even after the year (e.g. for sight, it is only 50% accuracy after 4 months). Customers believed that they spent 45 min. inside the store, while the actual time was 40 min. (odourless premises). Consumer perception changed after the introduction of scent – they thought they have spent only 25 min. in the store, with the actual time was more than one hour (Galeries Lafayette (Paris) – Scent search). And here are other examples how smell influences buying behaviour:
- After opening the store with chocolate „Hershey's „(New York, Times Square) the authentic scent couldn't be detected, because the chocolate was packed.
- Sales increased by 34% once the scent of chocolate spread throughout the store (Martin Lindstrom, Brand Sense).
- Consumer's opinion on shopping experience is greatly improved when the scent and background music are harmonized (Journal of Retailing, 2001).
- The perception of aromas combined with visual experience stimulates brain activity resulting in increased customer loyalty (Dr. Calvert, University of Warwick, England).
- People remember hundredfold what they smell compared to what they see, hear or touch (Sense of Smell Institute).
- Some tests show improvement in mood as much as 40% after the clients were exposed to pleasant fragrance (Sense of Smell Institute).

- Studies have shown that 84% of respondents prefer Nike pants bought in the store with scent than odorless stores and were even willing to pay about $ 10 more for the same pants! (Scent Marketing Institute).
- Studies in Samsung proved that 26% of buyers underestimate the actual time spent shopping while there is evidence that in areas with scent they spend up to three times more time (University of California – San Diego Chemosensory Perception lab, 2008).

(based on www.qex.sk/images/uploads/PREZENTACIA_VNEMOV_MARKETING.pdf).

6.3.5 Climatic conditions

Climatic conditions (temperature, humidity, dust and ventilation) are an integral part of the shops internal environment. The greatest influence on the shoppers has the temperature. Excessive heat can cause the fatigue of shoppers, which can reduce their concentration on the goods. Conversely, the low temperature shortens the time spent in the store. The temperature may cause the rate of concentration of the customers in the retail unit, and therefore it is appropriate to regulate the temperature separately e.g. in the area of fitting rooms (where the concentration of shoppers is increased), and in the rest of the store. Climatic conditions do not influence only the customers, but also on the sales staff and therefore they should complete the appropriate working environment (Bechiňová, 2010).

If there is a high concentration of carbon dioxide (CO_2) in the shop, customers are getting weak and sleepy and finally become discouraged from shopping. Fresh air contains approximately 400 ppm of CO_2 and its concentration in average room doubles in one hour. This applies for the stay of one person at rest. If there are more people who are, moreover, carrying out some physical activity (shopping), it is necessary to change the volume of the air in a room several times per hour in order to keep the quality of air.

6.3.6 Additional significant elements of the shopping atmosphere

In addition to the visual and sensory merchandising, other elements, which significantly affect the shopping atmosphere and are an integral part of the shopping environment, can be defined. These could be the design of the shop, the role of staff in retail units, the principles which should be respected due to the customer's purchasing behaviour and instruments of in-store marketing which can be used primarily for the sales support, but also to the completion of the shopping atmosphere.

Design and the arrangement of the retail unit therein generally include the inner and outer elements. The inner design factors include the shop equipment (store layout), personnel, used building materials, as well as lighting, music, colours, fragrance and climatic conditions.

The inner elements can also assign individual zones of retail space (sales area, area of cabins, etc.). The external elements are then characterized by the architecture and the retail unit's neighbourhood, the entrance to the store, the showcases, informational signs and parking areas. Attention must be paid to the selected elements of the stores design – to the architecture and surroundings of the retail unit, entrances, layout, checkout zone and the fitting rooms when it comes to interior elements of the stores design (Pražská and Jindra, 2002).

6.4 Application of neuromarketing in visual merchandising

Consumer psychology and neuroscience provide more detailed research on consumer behaviour and decision-making process at the point of sale. Dooley (2012) notes that modern neurosciences brought the tools providing an insight into human brains and thus opening a way to psychological process of decision-making – to the black box of brain. Recently, there is a strong interest in the concept of application of the neuroscience methods used for the research of consumer emotions and cognitive reactions. In fact, the use of psycho-physiological techniques in consumer research is nothing new. Observing of the eye pupil dilation and electro dermal activity (followed by eye tracking and measuring of cardiac activity) was carried out already in 1960 (Wang and Minor, 2008).

Bárta *et al.* (2009) state that it is necessary to pay attention to human behaviour while implementing the marketing, because shopping represents a comprehensive experience for human mind. New revolutionary techniques provide unimaginable potential for performance of marketing and neuromarketing techniques. Retail marketing is changing very quickly and many retailers are trying to use innovative ideas to help them to be different from their competitors (Hallbauer, 2008). Using sophisticated neuro-research, companies can uncover what influences their customers and what processes precede consumer's decision. Based on its results, companies choose an optimal marketing strategy directly at the point of sale. In this context, retailers can use merchandising and communication tools to attract customers' attention – POP and POS materials (Desir, 2014).

According to Genco *et al.* (2013), there are three basic tasks to be fulfilled by each retail unit in order to ensure that shopping will bring also comprehensive experience for consumer in addition to its practical aspect. All these tasks can be assessed with neuromarketing methods and benefit from its practical findings. Providing comprehensive enjoyment from shopping that includes finding, choice and payment can only be done if it in line with conscious and subconscious goals of the consumer.

Neuroscience research provides relevant answers to the questions in the field of visual merchandising and communication at the point of sale (Loewenstein *et al.*, 2008):

- ▸ attractiveness of the shop's exterior (storefronts, entries, banners);
- ▸ attractiveness of the shop's interior (design, atmosphere, illumination);
- ▸ attractiveness of merchandising and its tools (displaying, organization of goods, POP and POS materials);
- ▸ consumer behaviour and decision-making process at the point of sale (immediate vs planned purchases).

As stated by Berčík *et al.* (2014), neuromarketing research in the field of visual merchandising can be carried out in simulated or real purchasing conditions. This is related to the frequent use of mobile research technologies. Brain activity is mostly displayed by EEG, which is usually supplemented with biometric measurements such as EOG (measure with eye camera – eye tracker) and measurement of cardiac and respiratory activity (pulsemeter, HRV biofeedback and spirometer) (read more about it in Chapter 4; Berčík and Rybanská, 2017).

Under the application of neuro-displaying and biometric methods into practical research activities is understood their use in the research of selected situations in consumer behaviour. They provide information to be used for deeper understanding of consumer behaviour and decision-making. Nowadays, behavioural studies can be searched either in natural purchasing environment or simulated one.

6.4.1 Behavioural studies in natural purchasing environment

Observation of the mental state of buyers in natural environment falls into a range of challenges that are growing in proportion with more and more sophisticated and sensitive technologies for data collection. Following techniques are applied for carrying out the consumer neuro-tests in real purchasing environment:

Eye tracker: is a helpful method for analysis of consumer behaviour, POP and POS design and merchandising at the point of sale (Horská *et al.*, 2014). In this case it is necessary to use the mobile version of the device to ensure authenticity of the study.

Electroencephalography (EEG): provides very sensitive measurement of electric activity in brain but it is also very sensitive to muscle movements such as turning head, eye movements and other muscle activities. These signals endanger the EEG measurement of the person naturally moving in the shop. Same problem with disturbing elements can be found in biometric measurements of emotions based on the technologies using sensors applied on moving body (e.g. GSR, EMA).

6.4.2 Behavioural studies in simulated purchasing environment

It was found that consumer behaviour in real conditions can be transformed into laboratory conditions because deep subconscious processes and prejudices are activated in both cases. Eye tracker applied while testing the static pictures of planograms provides helpful knowledge on how the consumers visually browse the products displayed in shelves. If combined with other biometric and neurometric measurements and clear role of the selection, these studies can provide much practical information on the influence of various configurations of shelves when searching and choosing the products.

Compromise between reality and monitoring carried out within the testing of consumer behaviour can be achieved if customers are watching the video from purchasing environment directly in the laboratory. All participants of the test sample are watching the same video. This improves the control of testing and ability to stay in one position and disturbing elements become partly eliminated.

Imaginary walk in video recorded in shop aisles is another possibility for observation of the passive purchasing behaviour. Interactive virtual reality (VR) is used in order to create a shopping experience. Virtual purchasing environment brings significant savings in comparison to designing and preparation of tests in shop. In addition, it provides better balance between naturalness and control than can be achieved by watching conventional videos in laboratory.

Some neuromarketing agencies began to provide very detailed and interactive VRs including ideal 3D environment. In coming years, it is expected that this approach will be further developed as modern neuromarketing research tool.

Application of neuromarketing in visual merchandising in the retail can contribute to uncovering and understanding of real consumer preferences in grocery stores and significantly increase their competitiveness (Nagyová *et al.*, 2014).

Effectiveness and energy demand relates to the issue of effective presentation of products in retail stores. Especially, while using such important marketing tool as lighting, it is necessary to take into account energy consumption, because lighting is one of the main cost items of the retail store. The retailer should focus not only at the elegant presentation of displayed goods, but it is also needed to look for a compromise between energy consumption of lights and their influence on consumer perception at food market.

Energy consumption in individual retail stores may vary depending on format and segment. By far the largest energy consumption is in food stores to keep the food products in cold and also for presentation of the fresh products (Horská and Berčík, 2013). For this reason, neuromarketing can contribute with important information while choosing the material technical base. That creates a sufficient platform for combination of effective and efficient equipment of the retail store.

References

Alder, H., 2001. Mind to mind marketing: communicating with 21st-century customers. Kogan Page Business Books, London, UK, 252 pp.

Balnar, A., 2008. Příčiny a důsledky vlivu člověka na životní prostředí z fyzikálního hlediska. Ostrava-Poruba: Wichterlovo gymnázium, 56 pp.

Bárta, V., Patík, L. and Postler, M., 2009. Retail marketing. Cover design, Prague, Czech Republic, 325 pp.

Bechiňová, M., 2010. Fashion merchandising a jeho aplikace ve vybrané firmě: diplomová práce. VŠE, Prague, Czech Republic, 91 pp.

Bell, J. and Ternus, K., 2006. Silent selling: best practices and effective strategies in visual merchandising. Fairchild Books, New York, NY, USA, 399 pp.

Berčík, J. and Rybanská, J., 2017. Methods used in neuromarketing. Chapter 4. In: Horská, E. and Berčík, J. (eds.) Neuromarketing in food retailing. Wageningen Academic Publishers, Wageningen, the Netherlands, pp. 83-100.

Berčík, J., Paluchová, J., Kleinová, K., Horská, E. and Nagyová, Ľ., 2014. Stimulus, space and hidden customers reaction's: applying possibilities of neuromarketing research. In: Improving performance of agriculture and the economy: challenges for management and policy. Medzinárodné vedecké dni, Nitra, Slovenská poľnohospodárska univerzita, 138 pp.

Bhalli, S. and Anuraag, S., 2010. Visual merchandising. McGraw-Hill Education, New Delhi, India.

Borusiak, B., Pierański, B., Brohm, D. and Domurath, N., 2017. Application of neuromarketing in communication with the customer. Chapter 5. In: Horská, E. and Berčík, J. (eds.) Neuromarketing in food retailing. Wageningen Academic Publishers, Wageningen, the Netherlands, pp. 103-116.

Bosch, A.L.M., De Jong, M.D.T. and Elving, W.J.L., 2005. How corporate visual identity supports reputation. Corporate Communications 10(2): 108-116.

Custers P., 2010. Lighting in retail environments: atmosphere perception in the real world. Lighting Research and Technology 42(3).

Dannhoferová, J., 2012. Velká kniha barev: kompletní průvodce pro grafiky, fotografy a designéry. Computer Press, Brno, Czech Republic, 352 pp.

Desir, K., 2014. Better consumer understanding through neuromarketing in retail. Available at: http://tinyurl.com/ljmd35s.

Diamond, J. and Diamond, E., 2011. Conterporary visual merchandising and environmental design. Prentice Hall, Upper Saddle River, NJ, USA, 360 pp.

Dooley, R., 2012. Brainfluence: 100ways to persuade and convince consumers with neuromarketing. John Wiley and Sons, Mississauga, Canada, 286 pp.

Flynn, J., 1977. A study of subjective responses to low energy and nonuniform lighting systems. Lighting Design and Application 7(2).

Franěk, M., 2002. Psychosociální faktory ovlivňující úspěšnost environmentální výchovy. Sisyfos: Zpravodaj ekologické výchovy 1: 11-12.

Genco, S., Pohlmann, A. and Steidl, P., 2013. Neuromarketing for dummies. John Wiley and Sons, West Sussex, UK, 408 pp.

Hallbauer, S., 2008. Retail marketing and new retail idea – Marks and spencer. GRIN Verlag, Edinburgh, UK, 26 pp.

Horská, E. and Berčík, J., 2013. The influence of light on consumer's behaviour at the food market. Journal of Food Products Marketing 20(4): 429-440.

Horská, E., Mehl, H. and Berčík, J., 2014. Review of classical and neuroscience insights on visual merchandising elements and store atmosphere. Available at: http://tinyurl.com/n6nudfy.

Horská, E., Nagyová, Ľ. and Rovný, P., 2010. Merchandising a event marketing: pre produkty pôdohospodárstva. SPU, Nitra, 329 pp.

Horská, E., Paluchová, J., Prokeinová, R. and Moiseva, O.A., 2011. Vnímanie imidžu krajiny pôvodu potravinárskych produktov a aspekty ich kvality vo vybraných európskych krajinách. Slovenská poľnohospodárska univerzita, Nitra, Slovakia, 158 pp.

Kačmařík, M., 2015. Multimediální systémy. Available at: http://tinyurl.com/lg2987g.

Karlen, M., Benya, J. and Spangler, C., 2011. Lighting design basics. John Wiley and Sons, Upper Saddle River, NJ, USA, 256 pp.

Keaveney, S.M. and Hunt, K.A., 1992. Conceptualization and operationalization of retail store image. Journal of the Academy of Marketing Science 20(2): 165-175.

Kelly, R., 1952. Light as an integral part of architecture. College Art Journal 12(1): 24-30.

Kita, J., Kita, P., Konštiak, P., Oreský, M. and Vasiľová, M., 2012. Nákup a predaj: praktikum. Vydavateľstvo Ekonóm, Bratislava, Slovakia, 150 pp.

Kotler, P. and Armstrong, G., 1992. Marketing. Slovenské pedagogické nakladateľstvo, Bratislava, Slovakia, 385 pp.

Kotler, P., 1973/1974. Atmospherics as a marketing tool. Journal of Retailing 49(4): 48-64.

Loewenstein, G., Risk, S. and Cohen, J., 2008. Neuroeconomics. Annual Review of Psychology 59: 647-672.

Masson, J.E. and Wellhoff, A., 1985. Qu'est-ce que le merchandising? Dunod, Paris, France, 119 pp.

Mikula, M., 2015. QEX Vnemový marketing. Vplyv na správanie zákazníka v mieste predaja. Available at: http://tinyurl.com/m5t3l3s.

Morgan, T., 2011. Visual merchandising window and in-store displays for retail. Laurence King Publishing, London, UK, 208 pp.

Peglar, M., 2011. Visual merchandising and display. FairChild Books, Bloomsbury, UK, 432 pp.

Pradeep, A.K., 2010. The buying brain: secrets for selling to the subconscious mind, 1st edition. John Wiley, Hoboken, NJ, USA, 250 pp.

Pražská, L. and Jindra, J., 2002. Obchodní podnikání. Retail management 2. Management Press, Prague, Czech Republic, 874 pp.

Schiffman, L.G. and Kanuk, L.L., 2004. Nákupní chování. Computer Press, Brno, Czech Republic, 633 pp.

Šikl, R., 2012. Zrakové vnímání. Grada, Prague, Czech Republic, 312 pp.

Singh, A.S. and Kumar, R.S., 2015. Impact of visual merchandising on brand equity: an empirical study on premium apparel retailers. International Journal of Multidisciplinary Approach and Studies 2(6): 68-81.

Starzyczná, H., 2001. Ekonomika obchodu: Metodická příručka. Karviná, Czech Republic

Štetka, P., 2012. Scent marketing alebo aromamarketing. Útok predajcov na ďalší náš zmysel. Available at: http://tinyurl.com/l7nnf7f.

Viestová, K., 2008. Teória obchodu. Ekonóm, Bratislava, Slovakia, 7 pp.

Visual Merchandising / Window Dressing / Display. Available at: http://tinyurl.com/lpgjfkr.

Vymětal, J., 2008. Průvodce úspěšnou komunikací: efektivní komunikace v praxi. Grada, Prague, Czech Republic, 322 pp.

Vysekalová, J., 2012. Psychologie reklamy. 4. rozš. a aktualiz. vyd. Grada, Prague, Czech Republic, 324 pp.

Wang, Y.J. and Minor, M., 2008. Validity, reliability, and applicability of psychophysiological techniques in marketing research. Psychology and Marketing 25(2): 197-232.

Warren, M., 2005. Visual merchandising: digital technology has become a key element in bringing customers onto the site and into the store. Available at: http://tinyurl.com/lo2kclb.

Zielke, S. and Schielke, T., 2011. How store lighting influences store atmosphere, price and quality perceptions and shopping intention. In: Schielke, T. and Leudesdorff, M. (eds.) Impact of lighting design on brand image for fashion retail stores. Lighting Research and Technology 47(6).

7. Application of neuromarketing in visual merchandising in services

J. Paluchová*, J. Berčík and K. Neomániová

Slovak University of Agriculture in Nitra, Faculty of Economics and Management, Department of Marketing and Trade, Tr. A. Hlinku 2, 949 76 Nitra, Slovak Republic; johana.paluchova@gmail.com

Abstract

Visual merchandising is nowadays used and applied everywhere, from stores, public institutions, whole HORECA segment as well as in events. In business services, contact between provider and customer directly at the point of sale presents the most direct process of marketing, and time and money spending depend on atmosphere which is around the customer and influence his/her senses. The aim of visual merchandising is to capture consumer's attention. That means everything that customer can see, smell, touch, hear, exterior or interior, creates a positive or negative impact on a guest. Retailers or service providers are gradually realizing that only selling the product or services matters, but customers' satisfaction and convenience is too important for shopping. Visual merchandising is therefore concerned with both, how the product or service and their brands are visually communicated to the customer and whether this message is aptly decoded. The consumer perception is based on visual contact too; one picture can replace thousand words. Visual food merchandising is one of the hottest trends in the restaurant, foodservice and hospitality industry today, it is the modern art of presenting products in a way, that gets the guests to buy as well as bringing services to life with eye-catching displays of freshness, colour, quality, design, first impression or abundance. This chapter presents brief concept of visual merchandising applied in service sector, mainly meant in restaurants, coffee shops or teahouses. It also contains five senses of consumers and ways of influencing them by many marketing tools used in the connection to visual merchandising elements. At the end, we summarize application of neuromarketing techniques in practice of service providers using various visual merchandise elements that could be still improved, redesigned or changed with application of biometric or neuroimaging technics.

Keywords: restaurant, consumer senses, atmosphere, visual elements, neuromarketing techniques

Elena Horská and Jakub Berčík (eds.) **Neuromarketing in food retailing**
DOI 10.3921/978-90-8686-843-8_7, © Wageningen Academic Publishers 2017

Learning objectives

After studying this chapter you should be able to:
► Apply various merchandising tools in services
► Decide on neuromarketing methods, techniques, research plans and objectives to measure the impact of merchandising and point of service conditions on buying behaviour and decision to do purchase

7.1 Consumer and his/her senses in service marketing

Service marketing is a specific part of marketing and includes the process of selling various services (intangible products) as telecommunications, health treatment, financial, hospitality, car rental, air travel, and professional services are. Point of sale or point of service should be organized/arranged based on theory and principles of merchandising and sensory studies discussed in chapters 5 and 6.

Practical implementation 1

The Pasta & Grill's is located in Tenma Osaka, Japan where the various local restaurants and bars are dotted around the station. They serve tasty pastas and grilled beef and create the restaurant that looks like existing at the place long time. Painted brick-like wall and the use of antique tiles make us feel its history. By using the stripe patterns for some elements of the interiors, such as tent on the facade, fabrics for chairs, etc., they give the sense of urbaneness to the space. Guests experience the warm and relaxed atmosphere created by all those elements (The Pasta & Grill's by Dress, Osaka, Japan, 2014).

The coffeehouses in Slovakia began to be popular just few years ago (in the past Slovaks used to drink mainly home brewed coffee). The cafeterias are today very fashionable with various visual components. The popular concept of French or Italian coffeehouse is created with elements such as Italian or French music backgrounds or wallpapers with Eiffel tower. Of course, thematic coffeehouses offer also traditional cakes with different types of coffee. Elisabeth patisserie or GioCaffee in Nitra city invite the guests also with design and fashionable interior atmosphere with together with reasonable prices. In Elisabeth patisserie there is a bike as a component or wallpaper with cupcakes or macrons. GioCaffee offers various thematically created ice-creams (depends on the season) with the sofas and vintage designs store furniture. The patisserie is also known and promoted as the coffeehouse with the biggest playground in the city.

Coffee houses 'Urban House' and 'Urban Space' in Bratislava offer an unconventional concept of atmosphere with good coffee, choice of beer, quality wine, excellent cookies and other seasonings with outstanding music selection. They also serve as a club area with a stage and with events of various kinds. The atmosphere and interior is designed in hipster style. It is not only the fashion look, but the trend in gastronomy. The furniture is made from homemade pallets; the space is natural and easy. The atmosphere is most valuable, the coffee production in cafeteria cost few cents, but people are willing to pay more, because they pay for the space and atmosphere, where they are (Budaj, 2015).

Below you find some theoretical and practical issues and examples supporting idea of importance of consumer senses.

7.1.1 Sight

From using colours for their psychological triggers, to leveraging lighting, symmetry, balance, contrast, and focus to direct and control where a customer looks and for how long, it's one of the most fascinating components of merchandising. Warm yellow shades of light compliment gold jewellery as they add richness. Natural shades (daylight colours) are good for garments as they bring out the true colour of the merchandise. Bright colours like bright red or yellow are said to increase the pulse rate in human beings and trigger impulse purchases. The sensory stimulation is played by the type of lighting more or less fascinating. Sight is the most common marketing medium. Colour, architecture and graphic design theory are well-studied in the marketing industry and fill countless articles. It has been reported that visual elements can mould 90% of one's first impression. Colours, shapes, lines and textures all make up an image in the mind of the consumer. Also visual associations like cleanliness, crowds and food presentation all can impact the impressions (Bhalla and Anuraag, 2009; Caire, 2013; Horská and Berčík, 2013; Lindstrom, 2010; NeuroExpression, 2014).

Practical implication 2

From the American cuisine's restaurant named Parq San Diego (USA) and VIP services to the sound, lighting, and design, was created the ultimate experience with the latest technologies and advances in entertainment. The open-aired restaurant and lighted trees which are located in the middle of restaurant create a romantic and hip ambience. In 2015 won the award of 'Best atmosphere restaurant' organized by San Diego Magazine. The walls are lined with greenery and brick, and the faux jacaranda trees light up like constellations. Host truly feels like he is dining in the middle of a majestic European park on a perfect night.

7.1.2 Sound

The music played in store has a profound yet subtle effect on how customers behave in the store. Slow music keeps customers in a store longer. Music positively influences the perception of merchandise and service quality. Slow music can also lead to a rise in purchase rates. Researchers have found that the pace of background music affects customer perceptions of wait time, spending and turnover in stores and restaurants. Fast music decreases spending in a retail environment, but increases turnover in restaurants. Sound in restaurant can come from many forms including crowd noise, music, waterfalls and food sizzling. It can be a familiar jingle used in advertising or popular message received tones used in cell phones. Voices of people, movement of customers, background music, structures that isolate the different parts of the store offer solutions more relaxing and enjoyable, they communicate with the customer involving him, helping in the perception of the products (Caire, 2013; Lindstrom, 2010; NeuroExpression, 2014).

Practical implication 3

A fast-food is usually characterized by a high arousal level. There are many people, bright lights and loud, fast music. In contrast, the exclusive restaurant aims to create a relaxing atmosphere by providing dim lighting maybe using candle-lights, tables located at a comfortable distance from each other and slow background music. In the fast-food, loud and fast music is, among other elements, responsible for the high table turnover. In contrast, the relaxing atmosphere of the exclusive restaurant leads customers to stay after their meal and consume high-margin items (Ebster and Garaus, 2011).

7.1.3 Touch

The feeling, that consumer feels, is different with various types of flooring: rubber, carpet, ceramic or marble. The materials used for equipment, internal temperature and humidity are a factor that helps the customer to stay longer in the store. They also could try and touch the products. Consumer' hands are an important link between our brains and the world. People have more tactile receptors in little fingers alone than on entire back. These receptors help customer to explore objects in his surroundings. This sense of touch is referred to as our haptic sense. The skin is our largest organ and directly sends signals to the brain. (Caire, 2013; Lindstrom, 2010; NeuroExpression, 2014).

Practical implication 4

Disfrutar restaurant in Barcelona is interesting because of the entrance area which contains more urban references, like the metallic structures of the antique. The kitchen is the oven of the restaurant, both real and metaphorical as the guests can see the interior of this oven and see the cooking of meal. The guest can touch a food before eating, to control a quality of ingredients used for cooking. A wide luminous space is visually mimics the terrace and invites guests to open their gaze and spirit, transporting them away from the city to a more natural Mediterranean environment.

7.1.4 Smell

Smell is considered to be a fast track to the system in brain that controls emotion and memory, two very prominent factors behind why consumers choose one brand over another. The olfactory sense has the strongest influence on emotions as the olfactory bulb is directly connected to the limbic system, which is responsible for immediate emotional reactions. The scent evokes a spiritual presence, and recalls the nature of the soul. Essence and perfumes can make the environment more pleasant, inspire emotions, memories and moments that help to increase the desire. Even before seeing, the smell can stimulate us and bring back some situations. The human nose can identify and recall as many 10,000 aromas and as much as 75% of customer emotions are generated by what they smell. Scents can increase positive attention, mood and energy by 40%, but the reverse is also true. The smell makes the longest memorable sensation and emotion of flavoured environment, memory and brings in further visit. In gourmet restaurant and in wine store, aroma marketing is used minimally. This does not preclude the use of flavourings at the entrance to create a welcome effect, or where applicable in the toilet to create an aromatic filter (Caire, 2013; Ebster and Garaus, 2011; Lindstrom, 2010; NeuroExpression, 2014).

Practical implication 5

Fast food Dunkin' Donuts needed to address lovers of coffee in South Korea. Franchising is not connected with a coffee and because of that they hired the agency Cheil Worldwide that created campaign 'Flavor Radio'. In the buses, the passengers listen to the ad on the coffee in Dunkin' Donuts. The sound went together with coffee aroma directly in the buses. So, the people listen to an ad and smell aroma as well. Visiting of Fast food Dunkin' Donuts close to the bus stations increased over 16%. Together, this campaign attracted around 350,000 people and increased sales by 29%.

7.1.5 Taste

Taste can work magic in the business of selling consumables, giving people the chance to taste and sample before they buy is the equivalent of letting people try on clothes, a general and effective best practice. There are five flavours: salty, sour, sweet, bitter and spice. Taste mainly concerns food where the campaign tasted the most impact if the customer can taste the product before buying it. While of great importance to edible brands, doesn't fit well into the multi-sensory branding programs of other products. Of all the senses, taste is the weakest. In fact, taste generates the lowest emotional response. (Caire, 2013; Lindstrom, 2010; NeuroExpression, 2014).

> *Practical implication 6*
>
> The Starbucks' marketing strategy can be experienced with the five senses. The coffee smell has a certain something that makes guests feel comfortable, relaxed. It comes from fresheners placed strategically to invite guests to fancy a coffee in a very subtle way. The Starbucks 'music selection is a key in order to create an atmosphere that invites to relax while you are reading the newspaper, have a chat with your friends or even work with laptop. Starbucks' merchandising is placed close to the cashier areas, which allows customers to approach the goods while in queue and to touch them. Even at the risk of being stolen, Starbucks keeps its merchandising close enough to touch. The very well-known logo of the twin-tailed siren has accomplishment its mission to be recognised without the need to include the words Starbucks and Coffee. Guest eyes see the comfortable sofas that are part of the cosy design to reinforce the concept of a place between home and work (NeuroExpression, 2014).

7.2 Visual merchandising in services

Great visual merchandising is an essential part of sales strategy and through our survey we tried to evaluate the restaurant segment and opportunities for implementing visual merchandising components in selected restaurants. Visual merchandising engages all the senses, such as hearing, sight, scent, touch and taste. The more senses we engage, the more people respond to our operation, stay longer and buy more. It encompasses the way that the restaurants present their services to grab the customer's attention (Neomániová *et al.,* 2015). In full-service restaurants, the waiting area can incorporate design elements that serve as menu merchandising devices. Three environmental conditions make difference to customer comfort in the waiting area: light, temperature, and sound levels. Lighting levels must be controlled to provide a painless transition from outside space to interior space. Entering with an entrance facing west can be an optical assault, because going from bright daylight into a dim room is blinding. Temperature control in entry and waiting areas is a vital matter. Double sets of entry doors or revolving doors can prevent a blast of air entering the waiting area each time a customer enters. Most effective sound-absorbing materials are needed on ceiling and walls. Next to the options for a career in visual merchandising there are listed some related fields in service sector:

- ▶ Trade show/ exhibitions design: showcasing merchandise or products within a limited space. Visual merchandisers largely focus on lighting and other fine aspects of interior design.
- ▶ Food presentation: people first eat with their eyes. What looks good will most likely taste good? With newer cuisine and finer restaurants, wining and dining is breaking interesting ground.
- ▶ Product styling: adherence to a specific look or theme is necessary, as is the understanding of lighting.
- ▶ Events: every host wants the celebration to be unique and memorable.
- ▶ Malls: for such displays to be effective, they must be enhanced and exaggerated. Designing these huge promotional spaces for customers and window shoppers is a challenge.
- ▶ Restaurant planning: it's sea scope for visual merchandising, beginning with the façade and window display, to the aisle spaces and checkouts.
- ▶ POS point-of-sale materials: are contemporary and hence popular objects. It necessitates a good knowledge of material and design aesthetics. (Berčík *et al.*, 2015a; Bhalla and Anuraag, 2009).

Practical implication 7

Subconscious Pizza Hut menu knows what guest wants before he does. Pizza Hut has worked with tech firm Tobii Technology to produce the system what toppings guest want just by the way he's looking at the menu. Pizza Hut is using the table 'the Subconscious Menu' for its new gadgetry, a unique way to reinvent the dining experience. The menus are stripped-down, icon-based digital screens that feature 20 of Pizza Hut' most common toppings after just 2, 5 seconds, the table-style gadget is able to guess guest's favourite topping mix out of nearly five thousand combinations (Nield, 2014).

Level of restaurant services in Slovakia has undergone its development in recent years and there can be seen the number of positive changes. Customers become more demanding, allowing owners of catering establishments to face new challenges and adapt to the demands and requirements of their guests. Customer satisfaction today is not affected just by the quality and price of the offered food, but also by the entire range of offered services and the establishment atmosphere. The atmosphere is what often determines whether the customer will come back or not. For this reason, the examination of visual merchandising in terms of gastronomy has its important meaning. Surveys of several researchers show that customer expectations in restaurants and especially their emotional reactions are strongly influenced by the environment of catering facilities by itself. If the customer perceives the atmosphere positively, this is transferred by its positive attitude and expectations towards the quality of food and other services provided by the establishment (Jaini *et al.*, 2015). That's why creating a pleasant atmosphere and considering the various elements of the premise is crucial for the existence of any such entity. Classification of these elements was attempted by several authors, (Turley and Milliman, 2000) who divided them into external variables, general interior variables, layout and design variables, point of purchase and decoration variables, human variables as shown in Table 7.1 (Baker, 1987) who divided environmental factors into three categories which include ambient cues, design cues and social cues (Bohl, 2012).

In the restaurant industry, guests generally use food, physical environment and employee services as key components of restaurant experience in evaluating the restaurant service quality (Namkung and Jang, 2008) and eliciting restaurant image, guest perceived value, and satisfaction, which, in turn, affect guest behaviour. This combination (Table 7.2) of business attributes should result in guests' perceptions of high restaurant service quality, which in turn should enhance their satisfaction and loyalty.

Table 7.1. Ambient variables (Turley and Milliman, 2000).

External variables	exterior signs, entrances, exterior display windows, height of building, size of building, colour of building, surrounding stores, lawns and gardens, address and location, architectural style, surrounding area, parking availability, exterior walls
General interior variables	flooring and carpeting, colour schemes, lighting, music, scents, tobacco smoke, width of aisles, wall composition, paint and wall paper, ceiling composition, merchandise, temperature, cleanliness
Layout and design variables	space design and allocation, placement of merchandise, grouping of merchandise, placement of equipment, furniture
Point-of-purchase and decoration variables	point-of purchase displays, signs and cards, wall decorations, degrees and certificates, pictures, artwork
Human variables	employee characteristics, employee uniforms, crowding, customer characteristics, privacy

Table 7.2. Components of the physical environment (Baker, 1987).

Ambient factors	air quality – temperature, humidity, circulation
	noise
	scent
	cleanliness
Design factors	aesthetic (architecture colour style, materials, scale shape, texture, pattern)
	functional (layout, comfort, signage, accessories)
Social factors	customers (number, appearance, behaviour)
	service personnel (number, appearance, behaviour)

To explain the impact of these factors on behaviour of customers in the restaurant can be used SOR model modified by Mehrabian and Russell (1974) captured in Figure 7.1. According to this model the external environmental stimuli (e.g. music, scent, lighting, design, etc.) affect the emotional reactions of people (e.g. pleasure, arousal), which in turn impact consumer behaviour, e.g. desire to buy, the time spent in service, overall satisfaction, intention of repeated visits, etc. (Jang and Namkung, 2009; Ramlee and Said, 2014). We can explain this on example of the colours for example, that play an important role in the current visual merchandising restaurants. It is proven that warm colours stimulate, and therefore it is appropriate to use them in a case when we want to serve as many customers as possible in a short time as they are supporting the appetite.

Visual merchandising elements in the catering establishments can be examined through the traditional methods of marketing research but as well as using the neuromarketing techniques. For example within the neuromarketing research in conjunction with menu, it

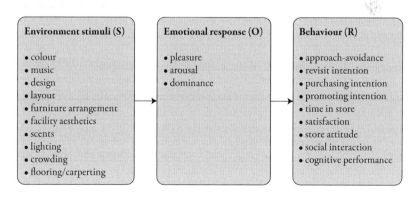

Figure 7.1. Influence of ambient variables (based on Ramlee and Said, 2014).

would be appropriate to focus on the overall design of the menu card or the wine card and then on its individual components: optimal number of items, configuration of items, using the different fonts, bordering of selected items, using pictures or photos of food in the menu, different displaying of the prices in the menu and so on. In connection with the lighting would be interesting to track customer behaviour by using different types and different colours of light to create culinary experiences reflecting either day or evening atmosphere. Similarly, it would be interesting to track impact of lighting via neuromarketing approach on customer behaviour using various musical genres, depending on the type of restaurant (luxury, fast food outlets, etc.).

Practical implication 8

During the rush hours of the day, lunch time, the McDonald's put adverts out that are specifically aimed at those driving a car. One advert for fries features a sound that you could describe as something like a deep fat fryer and the voice over even announces that the smell of fries being cooking and our mental representation of the smell of first, the customer are prompted to go and buy some. (NeuroExpression, 2014).

According to Kotler (1973) customers experience the atmosphere of the restaurant through a combination of visual (colour, lighting), sound (music genre, noise), tactile (purity) and olfactory (smell) elements. These elements can stimulate perception and emotional reactions of consumers and ultimately influence their behaviour. This statement is especially true for services including also investigated restaurants.

According to Pecotić *et al.* (2014) the interior design fulfils rather supporting function that can help restaurant to create unique image and distinguish the restaurant from the competition in order to increase customer's satisfaction, causing them to go back, disseminate good name of the restaurant and thus ultimately lead to increased income. Therefore, proper attention should be paid to restaurant's design and particularly consider the preferences and expectations of target customers so the whole restaurant would be perceived positively. Some restaurants use what researchers call decoys. They may place a really expensive items at the top of the menu, so that other dishes look more reasonably priced; research shows that diners tend to order neither the most nor least expensive items, drifting toward the middle (Bhalla and Anuraag, 2009; Chiasson, 2012; Green, 2013; RestaurantBusinessOnline, 2016).

7.3 Application of neuromarketing in service

Restaurants are great test labs for testing neuromarketing techniques. It's easy to change offerings, menus, and pricing, and one gets immediate feedback on what's working and what's not. In the visual merchandising for service' providers, there are elements, which affect the atmosphere and visualization of each store or retail that can be measured with neuromarketing techniques for improving services and influence the consumer decision. Neuromarketing techniques are based on scientific principles about how humans really think and decide which involves brain processes that our conscious minds aren't aware of. When combined with sound experimental designs and procedures, these new techniques provide insights into consumer decisions and actions that are invisible to traditional market research methodologies. Neuromarketing research can be conducted in the laboratory, but also in real conditions. Suitable biometrics methods must be selected, such as heart rate variability monitoring (HRV), eye movement (eye tracker), facial expressions (FaceReader) or neuroimaging methods, such as monitoring electrical brain activity (EEG) or a combination of these methods. Figure 7.2 and Table 7.3 list the major areas in restaurants, cafeterias or pubs, where neuromarketing is being applied today. The quality of research itself affects many aspects that need to be considered as overall fatigue of respondents or weather, representing the need to repeat these types of interdisciplinary research to obtain more accurate data.

Neuromarketing provides powerful techniques for measuring customer's brand association before entering the restaurant, from measuring the influence of restaurant's exterior to the employee uniform. Neuromarketing can measure consumer perception of interior decorations, chairs and tables design, positioning as well as location of food/ desserts in showcase, that are largely automatic, emotional and outside host conscious awareness.

In restaurants, neuromarketing has had a great success using colours to increase quest's appetite even further, even to find a way to make consumers leave fast. Some examples of this are red and yellow (colours that increase appetite), a very strong lighting as well as a very hard sound makes guest decide to eat quickly and leave. Effect of lighting on the purchasing decisions of consumers and the perception of lighting could be measured by using of EEG equipment in simulated or real conditions, to discover true consumer preferences for different lighting conditions (colour temperature, colour rendering index). And using a Colour and Lux Meters to measure the intensity and colour temperature of accent lighting used in restaurants/ cafeterias/ tea houses for the different kinds of drinks or food.

Neuromarketing provides powerful techniques for measuring customer's brand association before entering the restaurant, from measuring the influence of restaurant's exterior to the employee uniform. Neuromarketing can measure consumer perception of interior

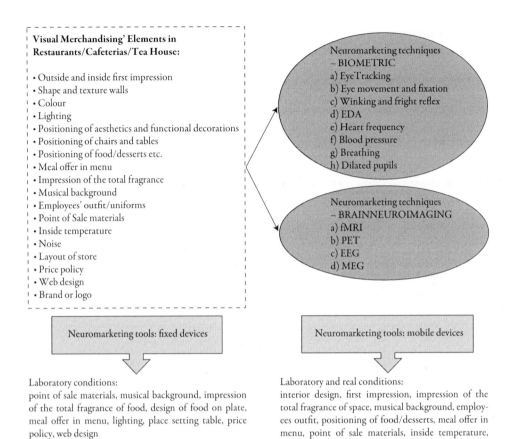

Figure 7.2. Model of potential elements of visual merchandising measured with neuromarketing techniques in the practice of restaurants, cafeterias or tea houses.

decorations, chairs and tables design, positioning as well as location of food/ desserts in showcase, that are largely automatic, emotional and outside host conscious awareness.

In restaurants, neuromarketing has had a great success using colours to increase quest's appetite even further, even to find a way to make consumers leave fast. Some examples of this are red and yellow (colours that increase appetite), a very strong lighting as well as a very hard sound makes guest decide to eat quickly and leave. Effect of lighting on the purchasing decisions of consumers and the perception of lighting could be measured by using of EEG equipment in simulated or real conditions, to discover true consumer preferences for different lighting conditions (colour temperature, colour rendering index). And using a

Table 7.3. Visual merchandising success factors.[1]

Visual merchandising elements	The most measured emotions in consumer behaviour and neuromarketing techniques in practice of restaurant/ cafeteria/ tea house
Outside and inside first impression	exterior and interior (eye tracking, EEG, GSR, EKG, laboratory: fMRI, MEG, PET, FMA)
Shape and wall texture	design and materials (eye Tracking, testing of forced withdrawals)
Colours	first impression, combination with lighting (eye tracking, EEG, GSR, EKG, laboratory: fMRI, MEG, PET, FMA)
Lighting	technical types and colours (eye tracking, EEG, GSR, EKG, laboratory: fMRI, MEG, PET, FMA)
Positioning of aesthetics and functional decorations	design and materials (eye Tracking, testing of forced withdrawals)
Positioning of chairs and tables	visible exposition of products and its right location (eye tracking, EEG, GSR, EKG, laboratory: fMRI, MEG, PET, FMA)
Positioning of food/ desserts	visible exposition of products and its right location (eye tracking, EEG, GSR, EKG, laboratory: fMRI, MEG, PET, FMA)
Meal offer in menu	price, weight, photos, allergens, visual background (PET, EEG, facial expression, eye movement and fixation, blood pressure, dilated pupils)
Impression of the total fragrance	inside and outside of pub, emotions (affective priming, EMG, Face Reader) association (fMRI, EEG)
Musical background	different style of music or sound inside (facial expression, heart frequency, fMRI, EEG)
Employees' outfit/ uniform	number of staff, behaviour, image, outfit (eye tracking, EEG, GSR, EKG, laboratory: fMRI, MEG, PET, FMA)
Point of sale materials	design and materials (eye tracking, testing of forced withdrawals), level of attention (eye Tracking, EEG), emotional reactions (EMG, analysis of facial expression, EEG)
Inside temperature	changing the temperature per day
Noise	measured with mobile application
Layout of place	product range and price offering (eye tracking, EEG, GSR, EKG, laboratory: fMRI, MEG, PET, FMA)
Price policy	discount or prices in selling zones, sale offer on the table (eye tracking, EEG, Face Reader)
Web design	on-line advertising (eye tracking, facial expression, EMG), using adaptation of web pages (eye tracking, EMG, EEG, fMRI)
Brand or logo	Association (fMRI, EEG), emotions (affective priming, EMG, Face Reader), motivation (behavioural studies, EEG)

[1] BVP = blood volume pulse; EDA = electro dermal activity; EEG = electroencephalogram, a brain-imaging method; EKG = electrocardiogram; FMA = facial movement analysis; fMRI = functional magnetic resonance imaging, oxygenation of the blood; GSR = galvanic skin response; MEG = magneto encephalography, magnetic field; PET = emission of positron.

Colour and Lux Meters to measure the intensity and colour temperature of accent lighting used in restaurants/ cafeterias/ tea houses for the different kinds of drinks or food.

In quick service restaurants, 75% of customers fully read the menu board after they order. Menus are printed marketing pieces, much like catalogues, magazine ads, etc., and some of the same techniques used in the latter media can be applied by restaurants. Profitable items or any items the menu designer wants to push can be emphasized with boxes, white space, graphic elements or, in some cases, a photo.

In case of music is important to consider the best possible matching of the intensity, frequency, music genre and tempo. Different pace can affect the rate of purchase, respectively eating time in the restaurant sector. The intensity and frequency of music can significantly affect the immediate emotional state of man.

The reasons why to apply neuromarketing techniques to the services sector and benefits of neuromarketing are as follows:
▸ Emotional-cognitive processing: neuromarketing can help to analyse the attention and cognitive processes which take place in the brain. It is clear that these work in a different way than has previously been suggested by the classic AIDA formula (Attention, Interest, Desire, Action).
▸ Neurolinguistics: to optimize text and language in menu or drinking card. To change the steps of food by price or weight in menu could help providers to find optimal way how to attract their menu.
▸ Neurosicentifics personality research: to identify certain consumer types, which can accordingly be segmented with greater chance of success through musical background (loud sound in bars or disco for younger consumers, slow music in coffee or tea house as well as an exclusive or traditional restaurants).
▸ Neuroscientifics gender/ age research: to determine the effects of differences in thinking style, emotional structure and behaviour for marketing purposes (women are more emotional, because could be measured impression of total fragrance or designing of food or desserts to arrange the interior style).
▸ Testing neuromarketing: number of choices on a web page, the picture of the product in menu, changing from a static picture to video, decreasing the number of food, drinks or desserts choices, the size of the headline, colour sets and wallpapers in houses or in the website design.
▸ Identify advertising elements: that trigger positive feelings, assess the logo and brands, images on the walls, price policy and music to develop advertising campaigns that are more appealing to consumers.

- ▶ Help avoid elements: that should not be present in the communication, such as elements that cause consumer aversion to the offered service: terrible aroma, noise or temperature, layout of place.
- ▶ Selection of visual features: as well as the timing and selection of appropriate media.
- ▶ Determine neural processes: are involved in the brain during the processing of brand information.
- ▶ Potential to identify the causes of purchasing disorders such as compulsivity through the listed visual merchandising elements in restaurants, coffee or tea houses.
- ▶ Determination of prices: a similar price level can be regarded in two different ways by the consumer. A high price for a given category of products/ services, for example, can be perceived as a feeling of loss and, therefore, prevent consumers from purchasing them
- ▶ Underlying consumption loyalty: in a study using fMRI, consumers had to choose the service brands they would like to visit and spend the time.

References

Baker, J., 1987. The role of the environment in marketing services: the consumer perspective. In: Czepiel, J., Congram, C.A. and Shanahan, J. (eds.) The services challenge: integrating for competitive advantage. American Marketing Association, Chicago, IL, USA, 108 pp.

Berčík, J., Horská, E., Paluchová, J. and Neomániová, K., 2015. Using of eye tracker in HORECA segment: visual proposal of chosen communication tool on restaurant guests decision. European Journal of Business Science and Technology 1(2): 93-103.

Bhalla, S. and Anuraag, S., 2009. Visual merchandising. Tata McGraw Hill Education Private Limited, New Delhi, India, 284 pp.

Bohl, P., 2012. The effects of store atmosphere on shopping behaviour. A literature review. Available at: http://tinyurl.com/lfd9m3s.

Budaj, J., 2015. Atmosféra je najcennejšia (Atmosphere is most valuable). Horeca Magazine 21.

Caire, G.G., 2013. Visual merchandising. Mirror and soul of a point of sale. Creative Group, Paderno Dugnano, Italy, 231 pp.

Chiasson, D., 2012. Foodservice and restaurant merchandising 101. Available at: http://tinyurl.com/kr5s2sy.

Ebster, C. and Garaus, M., 2011. Store design and visual merchandising: creating store space that encourages buying, 1st edition. Business Expert Press, New York, NY, USA, 150 pp.

Horská, E., Berčík, J. and Valach, V., 2013. Light quality and colour perception: a study on consumer reactions and environmental concerns in the supermarkets in Slovakia. Pangborn Sensory Science Symposium, 2013, Rio de Janeiro, 89 pp.

Jaini, A.B., Ahmad, N.A. and Zaib, Z.M., 2015. Determinant factors that influence customers' experience in fast food restaurants in Sungai Petani, Kedah. Journal of Entrepreneurship and Business 3(1): 60-71.

Jang, S. and Namkung, Y., 2009. Perceived quality, emotions, and behavioural intentions: application of an extended Mehrabian – Russell model to restaurants. Journal of Business Research 62(4): 451-460.

Kotler, P., 1973. Atmospherics as a marketing tool. Journal of Retailing 49: 48-64.

Lindstrom, M., 2010. Brand sense: sensory secrets behind the stuff we buy. Free Press, Houston, TX, USA, 192 pp.

Namkung, Y. and Jang, S., 2008. Are highly satisfied restaurant customers really different? A quality perception perspective. International Journal of Contemporary Hospitality Management 20(2): 142-155.

Neomániová, K., Paluchová, J., Berčík, J. and Horská, E., 2015. Visual merchandising and its marketing components in the chosen restaurants in Slovakia. Procedia Economics and Finance 34: 3-10.

Nield, D., 2014. Subconscious' Pizza Hut menu knows what you want before you do. Available at: http://tinyurl.com/m4sbrns.

Neuroexpression, 2014. But first, coffee. Available at: http://tinyurl.com/lqyss7x.

Pecotić, M., Bazdin, V. and Samardžija, J., 2014. Interior design in restaurants as a factor influencing customer satisfaction. RIThink 4: 10-14.

Ramlee, N. and Said, I., 2014. Review on atmospheric effects of commercial environment. Procedia – Social and Behavioural Sciences 153: 426-435.

Restaurant Business Online, 2016. 5 Trends likely to drive restaurant sales into 2016. Available at: http://tinyurl.com/n4hnbq7.

The Pasta & Grill's, 2014. The Pasta & Grill's by Dress, Osaka – Japan. Available at: http://tinyurl.com/kstbvuq.

Turley, L.W. and Milliman, R.E., 2000. Atmospheric effects on shopping behaviour: a review of the experimental evidence. Journal of Business Research 49: 193-211.

8. Future of neuromarketing

L. Loijens

Noldus Information Technology, Nieuwe Kanaal 5, 6709 PA Wageningen, the Netherlands; leanne.loijens@noldus.nl

Abstract

Neuromarketing is a hype, yet it is faced with a number of teething problems, including the costliness and complexity of its state-of-the-art techniques like electroencephalogram and functional magnetic resonance imaging. Such techniques require laboratory set-ups and so do not lend themselves to day-to-day market research processes. And neuromarketing still faces a number of other barriers. It still lacks supporting scientific proofs and it faces credibility issues as some early neuromarketing enterprises have made exaggerated, unverified and scientifically irresponsible claims. Additionally, most studies still rely on laboratory set-ups and expensive technologies which do not allow the necessary scalability for the techniques to be applied more widely. In order to overcome these obstacles, policy makers could make strategic initiatives and introduce ethical codes (EU, 2014). Yet as too many providers entered the neuromarketing field in its early days and failed to apply sound and robust scientific methods, a lot of credibility was lost. Although the methods applied nowadays have a more profound scientific basis, neuromarketing approaches still lack the scientific proofs that would support their case as meaningful methods and not just 'hocus-pocus'.

Keywords: ethics, issues, trends

Learning objectives

After studying this chapter you should be able to:
- Discuss further development of neuromarketing and its methodological, financial and ethical issues
- Discuss new trends in marketing and technology

Elena Horská and Jakub Berčík (eds.) **Neuromarketing in food retailing**
DOI 10.3921/978-90-8686-843-8_8, © Wageningen Academic Publishers 2017

8.1 The 'neuro' part of neuromarketing

8.1.1 More knowledge of brain functioning

For neuromarketing to grow we need more insight in the 'neuro' part, i.e. brain functioning. Although we know a lot about the brain and its functioning, there is still much more to learn. What we know today is just the tip of the iceberg. It is, for instance, well-known that the prefrontal cortex is involved in cognitive and emotional functions such as decision making, planning, social behaviour and impulse control (O'Reilly, 2010), but what does it say if we see activity in this part of the brain in an magnetic resonance imaging (MRI) scan? Data resulting from brain research are often explained in a simplified way for marketing purposes. Brain functioning is, however, not simple at all. And with complex stimuli, simple interpretation of brain activation is difficult. The more we learn about the brain, the more our insights change. It is not so long ago that it was assumed that the nucleus accumbens was the one and only centre for craving. Today we know that several other regions are involved (Schultz, 2000).

Finding a relationship between a certain brain area and behaviour (the kind of results neuromarketers are after) does not automatically mean that there is a causal relationship between the two. Many studies have shown that striatal activity correlates with hedonic rating scales. Neuromarketers have been quick to invert this finding and use ventral striatal activity as an indication that an individual likes something (a form of reasoning known as 'reverse inference'); but what is the evidence for this? Using a Bayesian analysis method (Poldrack, 2006) to analyse the BrainMap database, the posterior probability for a reward process was estimated given the observation of nucleus accumbens (NAc) activation. The prior probability of engaging in a reward-related process was assumed to be 0.5 (1:1 odds). According to this estimation, based on the number of functional magnetic resonance imaging (fMRI) papers reported in the BrainMap database with and without 'reward', and with and without NAc activation, NAc activation increases the probability of a reward-related process taking place to 0.90 (odds 9:1). This yields a Bayes factor of 9, which is considered moderate to strong evidence for a causal relationship. Although meaningful in a statistical sense, the assumptions behind such a calculation are rather liberal and may suffer from a publication bias for positive results, as well as differing definitions of reward. In real-world settings, the ability to infer whether an individual likes something based on NAc activation alone may be substantially less (Ariely and Berns, 2010).

Because of the reverse inference problem, using striatal and OFC (medial orbitofrontal cortex) activity as a read-out of 'liking' and the insula as a 'disgust-meter' is probably too simplistic to be of use in a real-life setting. In the context of neuromarketing, the statistical power of these single-region correlations may be too low for the correlations to be of use as predictors of consumption, unless, perhaps, the neuroimaging data is combined with other measures of preference.

The delusion of being able to look straight into the brain of the consumer by means of new imaging technology, thereby gaining access to his unconscious and secret desires will remain just that. Even though it is possible to identify brain areas responsible for particular feelings and thoughts, this does not provide information on what the consumer actually feels or thinks (Gentner, 2012).

Although some have argued for the existence of a 'buy button' in the brain, current evidence suggests that the cognitive processes associated with purchase decisions are multi factorial and cannot be reduced to a single area of activation. Conversely, a given brain region may be involved in multiple cognitive processes (Ariely and Berns, 2010).

8.1.2 The rational brain versus the emotional brain

It is not so long ago that marketers thought that you can convince people to buy something if you give them the right information about the product. Consumers were thought to be rational people who could be won over with good arguments. The idea that decisions are often made subconsciously and are based on emotions is relatively new (Kahneman, 2012). A few years ago, neuroscientists at the University of Iowa made a groundbreaking discovery which emphasizes the role of emotions in decision making. They studied people with damage in the part of the brain where emotions are generated and found that the patients seemed normal, except that they were not able to feel emotions. They all had something peculiar in common: they could not make decisions. They could describe what they should be doing in logical terms, yet they found it very difficult to make even simple decisions, such as what to eat (Bechara *et al.*, 2000).

Some popular neuromarketing books let us believe that we are helpless slaves of our emotions. The following blog post (www.eruptingmind.com/beating-the-reptilian-brain/) gives a good analysis of how emotions can control our behaviour: 'The influence of the emotional brain is most apparent when we do things we know we should not do and later regret'. For example, many dieters struggle to stick to their diet because they give in to 'temptation' and eat something that they said they would no longer eat. This occurs primarily for two reasons. The first is the natural pre-programmed response to food from the reptilian brain which readies the body to receive food. The second, and perhaps the most powerful, is the emotional association (memory) that has been linked to that food by the emotional brain. If the food is perceived as particularly tasty, and therefore pleasurable, the emotional brain strengthens the desire for food by activating memories associated with pleasure for that food. This can then result in real physiological bodily responses, such as salivation. Although your conscious brain may be telling you not to eat it because it makes you fat (logical response) somehow you suddenly seem to change your mind and eating the food does not 'feel' like such a bad idea anymore. After all, it won't hurt if you have just a little bit, right? (irrational response) Before you know it, you have eaten the food you were trying to avoid, and later, when the food is gone, your conscious thinking brain (which is no longer overpowered by the emotional brain) logically analyses your action leading to feelings of regret.

The old brain's control over buying decisions varies from culture to culture and from person to person. Fortunately for most of us the behaviour described above is an exception rather than the rule. We do not over-eat or make impulse purchases daily, we have a healthier balance between the emotional and the rational part of our brain.

It is a mistaken belief that non-conscious and conscious brain processes are somehow at war with each other. This is not the case. Instead of working against each other, our conscious and non-conscious brains operate as a very effective 'tag team' that, more often than not, keeps us on track to make good (or at least good enough) decisions throughout our everyday lives (Genco *et al.*, 2013).

8.2 Ethical, methodological and financial issues in neuromarketing

It is commonly accepted that traditional market research is flawed because consumers do not know, cannot articulate, or will even lie in a focus group about their purchase motivations. Many have thought that neuromarketing research removes subjectivity and ambiguity by going right to measuring observable brain behaviour. Now, and into the future, adopters of neuromarketing must keep in mind that non-conscious measures are not free of bias or confounds; they are simply novel techniques compared to consciously derived measures traditionally relied upon in marketing research.

Neuromarketing still suffers from the issue it is trying to overcome: the artificiality of market research. Brain activity in a lab may not equate to brain behaviour in the mall, where the buying decision is consummated. Although many eye trackers and physiological data measurement systems are wireless/wearable nowadays, the number of studies carried out 'in the field' (for instance, in a supermarket) are still limited. Test subjects still have to wear devices/electrodes/sensors, which may feel unnatural and may influence their behaviour.

Marketers, using neuromarketing techniques like fMRI, can look into the heads of consumers and investigate what drives people in their purchase decision. With this knowledge they could manipulate the consumer to buy products, and in the same session unravel political preferences, unmask covert racism, and distinguish truth from lies and even true love from mere lust. This ethical limit is a barrier to the development of neuromarketing and needs to be solved for neuromarketing to bloom.

Beyond the ethical side, the low use of neuromarketing is also due to other types of limits. There are methodological limits. Research protocols in fMRI studies are long and difficult to elaborate. For statistical power, a minimum of 10 repetitions within a stimulus category are required, although 20-30 would be more likely to achieve meaningful results. The number of subjects is generally weak. Apart from the simplest of tasks, any task invoking a response that is expected to vary across individuals, demands a sample size of at least 30. If groups of individuals are being compared under different treatments or conditions, the sample size will need to be much greater to detect differences between groups and between different treatments (Ariely and Berns, 2010). What may be even more important, techniques like fMRI can be unpleasant and uncomfortable for the subjects (noise, claustrophobia). Head movements are not allowed, subjects must stay still for at least 45 minutes up to an hour-and-a-half depending upon the complexities of the study, within an acoustically noisy scanner in a dark cool room (Ruanguttamanun, 2014).

To be able to run a study using neuromarketing techniques you need to be trained. Not only to carry out a study, but also to analyse the data. Several software packages exist to analyse neuroimaging data and although these programs make neuroimaging seem simple, it takes a minimum of 1 year of training to be able to use them and 3 years to become fully competent. And this not only applies to fMRI. Adopters of neuromarketing methods will increasingly require interpretation of new data types, not simply collections of indices or report cards of significant statistics. To that end, a new breed of client-side consumer insights professional will be required. These specialists will have the technical competency to access and apply non-conscious data beyond the reporting of a neuromarketing supplier in order to derive insights that are relevant in advancing company initiatives and ROI. Such trained personnel will be necessary in-house, or through access to consulting partners, who can take control of the massive amounts of data generated from such implicit techniques in order to convert the data streams into meaningful storylines and actionable insights. They will act as interpreters and integrators of bio-measures with traditional measures to uncover nuggets of insight that marketing and advertising industry executives can easily digest and apply.

And then there are legal limits. Neuromarketing studies like fMRI require a certain number of procedures since the subjects are submitted to brain imaging techniques. The agreement of an ethics committee, the wise consent of subjects as well as the assignment of a doctor as a supervisor is necessary to the conformity of the study.

In addition, neuromarketing suffers from financial limits. The costs of using brain imaging techniques are high. The cost of an fMRI scanner is between 1.0-1.5 million USD for a 1.5 tesla scanner and between 2-2.4 million USD for a 3.0 tesla scanner, an additional software cost is approximately $500,000 USD, and finally tops up with the cost of maintenance, specific room and the operation cost that can vary considerably, but generally fall somewhere between $400 and $3,000 depending on the facility (Ruanguttamanun, 2014). A neuromarketing study based on ten people can cost 50 thousand dollars or more. The high price of techniques is a major handicap to the progress of neuromarketing.

In spite of all these issues, the future of neuromarketing and the application of its academic sister, consumer neuroscience, in market research will continue to proliferate in applications and utility. Where once only the largest corporate conglomerates took the plunge in using tools that tap into the consumer subconscious, the value of neuromarketing will trickle down to smaller retailers and product manufacturers. Methodology that was once prohibitively costly with regard to timelines and budgets will become ever more attainable and on par with cost and turnaround times of traditional market research projects involving explicit measures.

8.3 Traditional marketing research methods are still valuable

Neuromarketing cannot replace traditional market research as the results from the brain studies are standard and open to interpretation to be useful in isolation. Both approaches complement each other and it helps taking both the explicit (what people say) and the implicit (how people subconsciously feel) into account.

Assessing brain activation is not generally useful without correlating it with some other measurement. It is necessary to have another behavioural measurement to anchor the interpretation of the brain activation. Be wary if someone claims to know what a person thinks based solely on brain activation (Ariely and Berns, 2010).

Marketers are increasingly enthusiastic about the promise of wearable tech and other emerging passive measurement techniques. But they are also looking for enhanced integration with more traditional methods that allow them to validate and contextualize the data they gather.

Surveys and focus groups are still necessary. When it comes to surveys, there are always some questions that are perfectly reasonable to ask people and that are likely to get accurate responses. Asking people to make rapid, simple, binary choices is a good survey technique. You only start getting into trouble if you ask people *why* they chose option A over option B, because the odds are, they have no idea – but they will make up something really good!

The best information conveyed by focus groups, is not what people say, but how they behave. Intuitive marketers can pick up these nuances and incorporate them as insights in their work. Ironically, just like intuitive consumers, intuitive marketers usually cannot articulate exactly how they do this or why or when it works (Genco *et al.*, 2013).

8.4 New trends in marketing and technology

8.4.1 Wearables

Today, the term 'wearable' goes beyond the traditional definition of clothing; it refers to an accessory that enables personalized mobile information processing. Wearable devices are wireless, portable/wearable sensors such as activity trackers, wireless electroencephalogram (EEG) caps, heart rate sensors, galvanic skin response (skin conductance) sensors, and wearable eye-trackers. At the moment, most of these devices are used for research and are not typical consumer wearables, but devices like smart-watches become more widely used and have better sensors and become more web-connected so the potential could be there to tap into useful data from these. A consumer wearable that is being worn by millions of people provides a big sample base, and then it just becomes a challenge of (1) gaining access to that user data, and (2) crunching the numbers. Some predict that the Apple Watch will track emotions within a few years, while companies like Humanyze already use wearable technology in tandem with social-media analytics to help employers know how their employees are feeling, physically and emotionally (http://www.humanyze.com/products. html). As we interact more with screens and 'smart devices' there will undoubtedly be increasing demand for those devices to understand human responses, to optimize themselves to our levels of interest, emotions, and behaviour.

A potentially pioneering technological advancement in neuroimaging is mobile fMRI. Researchers at the Technical University of Denmark developed the Smart Phone Brain Scanner (Stopczynski *et al.,* 2014). It combines low cost wireless EEG sensors with open source software for real-time neuroimaging. The scanner, which looks like a GPS but with a brain scan on it instead of a road map, is about the size of an adult's palm and can be worn almost like a headset used for playing an interactive Xbox game. The scanner is roughly 300 dollars and contains 14 electrodes that monitor your brain activity. The scans are then translated wirelessly onto a Nokia screen (or a tablet or phone presumably). One advantage of the technology is that it allows marketing studies and consumer research to be done anywhere, in places more similar to those where people would normally be exposed to marketers' messages, such as bars rather than labs.

One possible new brain-scanning technology that could be in wider use in 20 years is functional near-infrared spectroscopy (fNIRS). This is essentially a cap, like an EEG cap, that shines near infrared light through the skull then uses sensors to measure the diffusion of light through the brain to figure out which parts of the brain are 'working harder'. Currently, if you want to measure activity in the deeper regions of the brain you need to use an fMRI scanner. These scanners will likely improve in affordability and comfort in the coming years but fNIRS could be an even cheaper, more portable and less invasive alternative.

Hitachi has introduced a wearable brain scanner (Atsumori *et al.*, 2009; Funane *et al.*, 2011). The halo-like device is portable, allowing it to be worn while performing normal activities – perhaps even shopping. Devices like this provide vastly more freedom to interact with the environment than fMRI machines or other types of fixed scanning devices. The Hitachi wearable scanner uses optical topography to measure changes in blood flow to different areas of the brain – multiple laser diodes are used. It is interesting to see that a firm of Hitachi's stature is pursuing this technology.

One of the most powerful benefits of wearable technology is the gathering of personal data. For activity trackers, such as Fitbit and Nike Fuelband, this data is used by the individual to better understand and improve their health. For brands, access to personal wearable data could be used to improve the way they market and even develop their product and services to consumers. Recently, Toronto-based neuromarketing firm, True Impact Marketing teamed up with mobile application shop, Plastic Mobile, to understand the 'The Science Behind Mobile Design'. For the purpose of this study, they hooked up thirty participants with a Tobii Glasses Eye Tracker and Emotiv EEG Neuroheadset and had them move through the buying process on the Pizza, Best Buy and Hyatt Hotel mobile applications (True Impact Marketing, 2014). As wearables with the same measurement capabilities get into the hands of everyday consumer (Google Glass, Muse, to name a few), brands may be able to simply tap into this data. We may even see a time when users grant permission for brands to access this information in lieu of loyalty incentives as we do with our online behaviour now.

8.4.2 Augmented reality

Another new trend in marketing is augmented reality. Augmented reality is a technology that adds an extra layer of virtual information on top of the perception of the real world, in real-time. Usually the virtual layer consists of 3D objects or 3D scenes, with or without sound. Sometimes only textual info is added. Everyone, from shoppers, tourists, to someone looking for the closest subway stop can benefit from the ability to place computer-generated graphics or text in their field of vision.

Researchers at IBM Labs have made an augmented reality shopping app (IBM, 2011). The app, which is being developed by IBM's Research lab in Haifa, Israel, does not rely on barcodes or RFID tags to recognize products, but instead uses the camera of a mobile device and compares the image to a database of product packaging. The image processing algorithms combine techniques used in facial recognition, colour and shape matching, and associations with surrounding products. The app also takes into account the camera angle and distance from the product to help distinguish between products. Once the product is recognized, the app will then overlay digital details of the product on the image. This can include nutritional information, price, reviews and discounts on offer at that time. Consumers can also choose to opt into a social networking feature that would see comments or reviews from friends and family about a particular product added to the information displayed. While shoppers get instant access to the wealth of product information available online, retailers would also benefit. They can use the app to attract customers back with the use of loyalty programs and digital coupons, while also gaining an understanding of customer preferences that would enable them to suggest related products in other aisles.

Augmented reality is also seeping into the publishing sector. The December 2014 issue of South Africa's most established food magazine, Food & Home Entertaining, has augmented reality added (Food & Home Entertaining, 2014). Thanks to generous sponsors at SPAR, the Dutch multinational retail chain, this edition offers readers 18 pages of interactive content, which can be viewed by simply downloading the free Layar app from the Apple App Store or Google Play and scanning each page that features the Layar logo on it. Readers are able to access the magazine's stock of tasty recipes which has many how-to videos. Readers are also afforded the opportunity to win their share of thousands of rands worth of vouchers and hampers.

8.4.3 Virtual reality

The step from lab studies to tests in real-life environment like shops and people's kitchen is often difficult in neuromarketing. It may, therefore, be helpful to simulate real-life environments with virtual reality techniques. A good example is the 'virtual shop simulator' that is being developed in the FOCOM (Food and Cognition Model systems) project, a research project financially supported by the European Fund for Regional Development, the province of Gelderland and the Dutch national government with a total budget of € 8.4 million. The concept of a virtual supermarket is not new. There are several companies and institutes that already developed such a supermarket. Examples are the virtual shops developed by Green Dino (www.greendino.nl/virtual-labs.html), Tesco (http://tinyurl.com/kvq4xff) and GfK (http://tinyurl.com/mxfn586).

The virtual shop simulator currently being developed in the FOCOM project allows a consumer to navigate through a virtual supermarket while his behaviour, physiology and brain responses are captured. A translation will be made from a clinical fMRI environment to a more relevant test environment in which eye movement and brain responses such as EEG and NIRS (near-infrared spectroscopy) can be measured. The technique is being used to investigate why consumers like or dislike certain products, and how the choice and purchase process works. Special attention will be paid to the influence of the design of product packaging on choice behaviour.

References

Ariely, D. and Berns, G.S., 2010. Neuromarketing: the hope and hype of neuroimaging in business. Nature Reviews Neuroscience 11(4): 284-292.

Atsumori, H., Kiguchi, M., Obata, A., Sato, H., Katura, T., Funane, T. and Maki, A., 2009. Development of wearable optical topography system for mapping the prefrontal cortex activation. Review of Scientific Instruments 80(4): 043704.

Bechara, A.; Damasio, H. and Damasio A.R. (2000) Emotion, decision making and the orbitofrontal cortex. Cerebral Cortex 10 (3): 295-307).

European Union (EU), 2014. Directorate-general for enterprise and industry. Customer experience, neuro-marketing innovations. Business innovation observatory. Contract No. 190/PP/ENT/CIP/12/C/N03C01. Available at: http://tinyurl.com/m3f3u42.

Food & Home Entertaining, 2014. Available at: http://tinyurl.com/l2bwmnx.

Funane, T., Kiguchi, M., Atsumori, H., Sato, H., Kubota, K. and Koizumi, H., 2011. Synchronous activity of two people's frontal cortices during a cooperative task measured by simultaneous near-infrared spectroscopy. Journal of Biomedical Optics 16(7): 077011.

Genco, S.J., Pohlmann, A.P. and Steidl, P., 2013. Neuromarketing for dummies. Wiley and Sons, New York, NY, USA, 408 pp.

Gentner, F., 2012. Neuromarketing in the B-to-B-sector: importance, potential and its implications for brand management. Diplomica Verlag GmbH, Hamburg, Germany, 82 pp.

IBM, 2011. Augmented reality makes shopping more personal. Available at: http://tinyurl.com/lagzzdf.

Kahneman, D., 2012. Thinking, fast and slow. Penguin Books Ltd., London, UK, 512 pp.

O'Reilly, R.C., 2010. The what and how of prefrontal cortex organization. Trends in Neuroscience 33: 355-361.

Poldrack R.A., 2006. Can cognitive processes be inferred from neuroimaging data? Trends in Cognitive Science 10(2): 59-63.

Ruanguttamanun, C., 2014. Neuromarketing: I put myself into an fMRI scanner and realized that I loved Louis Vutton ads. Procedia Social and Behavioral Sciences 148: 211-218.

Schultz, W., 2000. Multiple reward signals in the brain. Nature Reviews Neuroscience 1: 199-207.

Stopczynski, A., Stahlhut, C., Petersen, M.K., Larsen, J.E., Jensen, C.F., Ivanova, M.G., Andersen, T.S. and Hansen, L.K., 2014. Smartphones as pocketable labs: visions for mobile brain imaging and neurofeedback. International Journal of Psychophysiology 91(1): 54-66.

True Impact Marketing, 2014. The science behind mobile design. Available at: http://tinyurl.com/l6ju4dz.

Printed in the United States
by Baker & Taylor Publisher Services